THE (

Being hurt and heartbroken is a sad reality for most of us. But I'm so thankful for this treasure of a book written by my friend Suzie Eller. Page by page, Suzie will help you understand how God's truth can heal your pain so you can move forward whole and healed.

LYSA TERKEURST
New York Times Bestselling Author
President of Proverbs 31 Ministries

If you've ever felt too broken for God to fix, then *The Mended Heart* is for you. Suzie Eller takes you by the hand and guides you step-by-step toward the only Source that offers complete wholeness. Each chapter exclaims, "There's no hurt God can't heal." Do yourself a favor—read this book!

MICCA CAMPBELL
Speaker, Proverbs 31 Ministries
Author, *An Untroubled Heart*

The message of *The Mended Heart* is especially uplifting. The author beautifully emphasizes the redemptive power of Jesus and his glorious triumph of overcoming the plight of this world—a much-needed message to those carrying the burden of their personal sufferings. As a biblical counselor, I repeatedly come face-to-face with clients bearing the weight of their own brokenness and in need of a "mended heart." Readers who have ever known strife caused by adversity and worry will find this book to be an invaluable read as they discover the battle has been won by what Jesus has already done for us on the cross.

CHRISTINA CALK
Board Certified Biblical Counselor
Family Pastor at Praxis Community Church

The Mended Heart is part challenge, honest storytelling and deep, deep encouragement for anyone who has experienced loss, betrayal or pain. Eller acts as a gentle guide, shepherding you through your pain to find wholeness and purpose on the other side. Tenderly told, and filled to the brim with Jesus, this book will prove to be a blessing to many.

MARY DEMUTH
Author, *The Wall Around Your Heart: How Jesus Heals You When Others Hurt You*
Blogger at *Your Life Uncaged*, MaryDeMuth.com

If you have experienced a broken heart due to pain, disappointment and hurt inflicted by others or because of your own wrong choices, read this book. In *The Mended Heart*, Suzie Eller reveals life-changing biblical principles and answers the tough questions we are sometimes afraid to ask. The "Just You and God" section will lead you step-by-step on a journey to healing. Don't miss this important book!

CAROL KENT
Speaker and Bestselling Author, *When I Lay My Isaac Down* and
Unquenchable: Grow a Wildfire Faith That Will Endure Anything

"What You Don't Have to Do," the first chapter in Suzanne Eller's *The Mended Heart*, hooked me. It wasn't one of those books that gives simplistic formulas to solve all problems and makes us feel guilty because they don't work. Eller writes with a warm sensitivity as she touches the wounded places. She writes with a compassion that helps us cope with the worst of pain—always reminding us that God's love mends our hearts.

CECIL MURPHEY
Author or Co-author of more than 130 books, including
I Believe in Heaven and *I Believe in Healing*, and bestsellers *90 Minutes in Heaven*
and *Gifted Hands: The Ben Carson Story*.

In *The Mended Heart*, Suzanne Eller holds her readers' broken hearts in tender hands as she layers on healing truths about Jesus, the Healer. She skillfully communicates both the realities of our hurts—whether self-inflicted or caused by others—and the undeniable Hope for living whole again. Hope with a name—Jesus. Don't skip the questions and answers at the end of the book. Eller's empathy and practicality shine brightly in these "Q&A" pages.

CYNTHIA RUCHTI
Speaker and Author, *Ragged Hope: Surviving the Fallout of Other People's Choices*

SUZANNE ELLER

Speaker Proverbs 31 Ministries

THE *Mended* HEART

GOD'S HEALING FOR YOUR BROKEN PLACES

Revell

a division of Baker Publishing Group
Grand Rapids, Michigan

Published by Revell
a division of Baker Publishing Group
PO Box 6287, Grand Rapids, MI 49516-6287
www.revellbooks.com

Revell edition published 2014
ISBN 978-0-8007-2495-5

Previously published by Regal Books

Printed in the United States of America

Library of Congress Control Number: 2014955803

Published in association with Books and Such Literary Agency, Santa Rosa, California.

For privacy, the names of some of the people profiled have been changed. Permission has been granted for personal stories used throughout.

15   16   17   18   19   20   7   6   5   4   3   2

Dedication

I dedicate this book to my Savior, whom I rediscovered all over again
in a small community prayer room in Fayetteville, Arkansas. His presence
wrapped around me as I read and researched His story, and as I prayed that
He might show me what it means to live in His mission statement so that we
might be made whole. I celebrated His response to flawed and hurting humanity,
and how knowing Him and being known is such a gift.

I want to thank Richard, my husband. Who knew that when you saw that
girl sitting in her Mustang, her hair flying in the wind, that we'd still be on an
adventure 34 years later? Thank you for understanding and championing this
call on my heart. You encourage me and offer grace when deadlines loom.
You are my friend, my love, and a man who knows Jesus well.

To Leslie, Stephen, Melissa, Josh, Ryan and Kristin, you are some of my
greatest cheerleaders. I'm so grateful for adult children who not only love to
spend time with their mom, but who also encourage me to pursue all that
God has placed on my heart.

To my grandbabies: Elle, Luke, Jane, Audrey and Josiah.
Having five grandchildren ages three and under is not only crazy fun,
but it's also a blast! Twenty-three years ago, when I heard the word "cancer,"
I didn't know if I would see my own babies grow up. To have your
little arms wrapped around my neck is sheer joy.

And to my mom, Karen Morrison. I love you like crazy.
Now we can have a lunch date!

*I also want to thank Rachelle Gardner,
my Books and Such agent. Thank you for partnering with me.*

*Thank you to Kim Bangs and Regal. How lucky I am that my editor
and publisher are friends who pray for their authors, who continually encourage,
and who show their love for Christ in their excellence and work! Special thanks
to Kim, Jackie and Tasha, who selflessly work behind the scenes
so that these words can reach as many as possible.*

*I also want to thank the women who served as a focus group as I penned
these words. Thank you to Jennifer, Jill, Julie, Gloria, Sarah, Tracie and Amy.
You didn't blink when I scrapped the first three months of work to start fresh.
You simply jumped on board and started over with me. Thank you for reading
each chapter, for being honest, and for sharing those "a-ha!" moments when
the text touched you personally, as well as those "oh no!" moments
when I needed to dig in a little deeper.*

*Last, I want to thank you, the reader.
When you show up on my blog (www.tsuzanneeller.com)
or on Twitter or Facebook, or you send an email, it tells me that
all the words written in a little coffee shop didn't just disappear
into thin air. I love that we pray, explore God's grace,
and discover healing together. What a privilege!*

Contents

Foreword

As a young mom, I wore fear, worry and anxiety around me like a heavy old robe. I had three young boys and battled a disease that left me exhausted and constantly frustrated. Even so, I enjoyed sweet times of fellowship with God. I pursued Him, ran after Him with a passion and zeal. I pulled myself out of bed in the mornings before the boys got up so I could have some time in the Word, time in prayer and time to listen to what the Lord had to say to me. He really was my greatest treasure, even though up to that point my life was nothing like I thought it would be.

I struggled more often than not. I hated my fears and insecurities; I wondered if I'd ever get free from the past pain that plagued me so, or if God would ever deliver me from the sickness that sapped me of my strength. I finally cried out to God in the most reckless way, "Lord Jesus! I can't pursue You more than I do right now with three little kids and this wretched disease! I pray. I read. I journal. I spend time with You. But when I get up from this place, my life seems no different. I still battle the same fears and insecurities. What am I missing, Lord? Where's the victory?"

I waited.

Then He spoke to me:

I get that you love Me. But you don't seem to understand that I love you. So from now on—until I tell you differently—every time you're about to say, "I love You, Lord," I want you to turn it around and say, "You love me, Lord." Say it now.

Shocked and surprised by this revelation, I whispered under my breath, "You love me, Lord."

He whispered to me again, *Say it again.*

"You love me, Lord." I repeated this statement several times and had to admit, something about those words seemed both foreign and familiar—foreign because I'd put more emphasis on my walk with God than on His walk with me; and familiar because I realized that He designed me *for Him*, to be loved by Him, to walk with Him, so that *living in response to that love* would become the most natural, supernatural thing in the world.

Scripture tells us that God loved us first. While we were *yet* sinners, He died for us (see Rom. 5:8)—that it's not about how high we can jump, but that He stooped down to make us great (see Ps. 18:35). And that "it is *for freedom* that Christ has set us free" (Gal. 5:1, emphasis added).

We've all been bruised and battered by this life. People hurt us and we make our own bad choices; and, for far too many, that's where the story ends. But it doesn't have to be that way. There's a way to get unstuck, a way through the valley and to the other side.

God extends His hand to you on this journey and, if you trust Him, He'll do such a deep work in you that you'll barely recognize yourself once the story is over.

My friend Suzie Eller has written a book that invites you to take those steps toward healing today. She'll hold your hand, speak life to your soul and remind you of many important things, like:

You are not alone.
You don't have to earn God's love.
You don't have to run anymore.

Suzie will teach you the wonder of a changed perspective—how when you shift your focus from what you do to what Christ has already done, that's when the healing begins. His finished work for you is enough to save you, *and heal you.*

Suzie is a wise woman of God with oodles of life experience. She oozes the love of God because she walks intimately with Him. Her greatest passion is to see others healed and restored and mobilized to be and do everything God intended for them, because that's what God has done for her.

Listen to this friend of mine. She speaks with wisdom and authority and compassion. Your healing journey truly is about to begin.

May God surprise and bless you with rich and deep revelations of His love in the days to come.

Susie Larson
Radio Host, Author, Speaker

PART 1

What Jesus Has Already Done for You

Jesus' Mission Statement

"The Spirit of the LORD *is upon Me,*
Because He has anointed Me
To preach the gospel to the poor;
He has sent Me to heal the brokenhearted,
To proclaim liberty to the captives
And recovery of sight to the blind,
To set at liberty those who are oppressed;
To proclaim the acceptable year of the LORD.*"*
Then He closed the book, and gave it back to the attendant
and sat down.
And the eyes of all who were in the synagogue were fixed on Him.
And He began to say to them,
"Today this Scripture is fulfilled in your hearing."

LUKE 4:18-21, *NKJV*

Introduction

"I am anointed to preach the gospel to the poor,
to heal the brokenhearted, to preach deliverance to the captives,
to give sight to the blind, and to set at liberty those who are bruised,"
Jesus said in the most magnificent Mission Statement ever conceived.
And He fulfilled it perfectly, exquisitely, completely.

JON COURSEN[1]

Whenever I meet a woman with broken places in her heart and being, I almost immediately begin to wonder what she will look like in the hands of our Savior.

What will He do in those broken places?

In what ways will His touch change the direction of her life?

Who is she destined to be with a heart made whole?

Considering the possibilities excites me. For Jesus came to heal the brokenhearted! In fact, our healing was part of His self-proclaimed mission statement (see Luke 4:18). He stood in Nazareth—His boyhood hometown—as He proclaimed those words. The crowd looked at Him and saw a carpenter's son. Some questioned. Others walked away. Yet those who dared to believe discovered that knowing Jesus transformed their lives.

Those who accepted Jesus' proclamation as truth put their feet on a new path. Even though Jesus' mission statement was a fulfillment of the teachings they had studied all their lives, it challenged everything they had ever been told. This proclamation was hard to grasp, because it led them away from a tradition-based religion to the premise of an intimate relationship. It challenged the idea that they had to earn or work their way into faith. Instead, they were asked to accept that they were on God's mind to such a degree that compassion came in the form of a Savior who was willing to shoulder a burden they—and we—weren't equipped to carry.

Jesus stood in front of the crowd that day prepared to embrace a cross that would remove our sorrow and replace it with peace. This obedient sacrifice placed Jesus' feet on a road that led to suffering for Him—but had a destination of healing, restoration and redemption for each of us.

Jesus' message needed to be spoken then, and it's just as powerful today. It's a message that, if you embrace it, will challenge you to seek beyond what you see and feel, to find the Luke 4:18 thread running through your faith and inside of you.

Years ago I spoke at a small church. Afterwards two women approached me. They could almost pass for twins, except for the scars borne by one.

"She rescued me," the younger sister said. "She drove through the night, even after I told her to stay away. She made me leave with her. I would be dead today if she hadn't."

This woman had filled her broken places with a man who fractured not only her heart, but also her bones. Even after her sister whisked her away in the dark of night, she didn't know how to begin to heal. She wasn't sure if God even knew that she existed.

"Can we pray?" I asked.

She knelt eagerly, pressing her forehead into my knees. She wrapped her arms around my legs before I could kneel beside her. Years of loss, pain, and a chasm so wide she feared there was no way back bled through her tears.

It is in moments like this that I realize how human I am, and how little I truly have to offer.

But God.

As we prayed, I placed my hands gently on her head and asked God for what felt impossible in the natural. I cannot explain the presence that filled that small space. It was a tangible, almost overwhelming compassion of a Savior for His beautiful daughter.

Now, this might be the point where you say, "My life doesn't look like that. Perhaps this isn't the book for me."

There is brokenness that is easy to see, like that of a woman marked by abuse or of an addict perched on a sizzling sidewalk. But brokenness has many faces. It's found in the heart of a 30-something woman who thrusts a photo of her handsome husband and a little girl with a sweet baby-tooth smile into my hands and whispers, "I just can't keep feeling this way. I want more for them. I need more for me."

It's found in those who have been abused by a church doctrine or by parents who mixed Christianity with harsh or damaging theology. It's the mark on the heart of a mother who held her young daughter in her arms as breath left her child's body. It's found in the woman whose life turned upside down when her husband left her.

Brokenness can result from discouragement and unmet expectations—in plans that fly far astray from the way you thought they would go; from events you didn't see coming and couldn't prevent even if you did; from the choices of your past—or the choices of others that brought pain into your life. We could focus on how the brokenness came to be, but what might happen if we turned to the promise found in Luke 4 instead?

Every story is unique—and each story, including yours, is important. In the pages of this book, we'll meet women who arrived at brokenness from vastly different starting points. But brokenness does not have to be the end of any of our tales. When we couple our stories with the Jesus Factor, we are offered the beautiful gift of a mended heart.

Now, when Jesus shared His mission statement, those standing in front of Him were familiar with the origin of the words (see Isa. 61:1-2), but they didn't necessarily know how to apply them. Their parents and grandparents and great-great-great-grandparents had talked about the Messiah who would one day arrive. But they were looking for a King, not a heart surgeon.

They were awaiting a sword-carrying, chariot-driving God of power and might who would rescue them from the nations that oppressed them and avenge them of misdeeds done to the nation of Israel. They didn't recognize that the prophecies actually depicted a Savior who came specifically to open blind eyes, set prisoners free, mend broken hearts and the bruised spirits of His sons and daughters, and bridge the gap that divided man from the freedom of an oh-so-personal relationship with their Creator.

Though they didn't quite grasp it, Jesus fully understood who He was and why He had come—and who was on God's mind when He sent Him.

Maybe you've been searching for healing for a long time. You recognize brokenness because you *feel* it. Perhaps you have come to identify yourself as broken, or maybe others have tossed about that word when they describe you. Put yourself in that hopeful crowd. Hear what Jesus is saying to you. Those words spoken in the synagogue in Nazareth have your name on them. You can never be so broken that He can't put the pieces back together. Your broken or wounded places may have caused you to feel "less than"—but to our heavenly Father, healing your heart is the very reason Jesus was sent. God's promise of healing is for you if you've been asking these questions:

What's wrong with me?
Why can't I get past this?
God, do You even see me?

When you realize that Luke 4:18-21 is for you, it creates a brand new set of questions. But we'll look at only one at this point of your journey:

What miracle does my God desire to perform in me?

I believe in miracles, because I am one. Jesus transformed me from a fractured, insecure, hurting young woman into a strong woman of faith, a mom, a wife, and a grandma to five beautiful babies.

Long after my initial encounter with Christianity, my Savior has been my Refuge and my Healer in those times when life has hit so hard that it feels as if my breath has been taken away. He's a Rock so secure that I am able to stop running from brokenness and instead run toward my God and all that He has in store for me.

When we grab hold of Jesus' personal mission for us, something profound begins to take place. We become an integral part of the good news. The apostle John says this:

> Jesus did many other things as well. If every one of them were written down, I suppose that even the whole world would not have room for the books that would be written (John 21:25).

Yes, there are 66 books in the Bible. But the story of God's people is still being written. As we walk with Him, we become the new books that might never be canonized but that proclaim the power of Jesus for others to see. What a beautiful story these living books tell—and what a wonderful gift they are to those who hear them! When we've experienced brokenness, and Jesus has healed our hearts, we can't help but come alongside others who are walking where we once walked, joining an army of strong women of faith to tell the world that there is a place beyond brokenness.

May I share something with you as we start this study together? Sometimes miracles are instantaneous: The person who could not walk suddenly leaps to her feet and dances away, all her troubles behind her. But for most of us, it's a process.

Embracing Jesus' mission statement might require going against your feelings. It's a trust walk—both on days when you feel it and on those days when you trust God despite your feelings. It's not always easy, but things of great value rarely come without personal discovery, exploration, insight and renewed direction.

Even as God works in you, you will still be human and fallible. You won't please everybody with your progress or the rate at which it takes place. At the end of it, you might not even look like a perfect church girl (which is okay—it's not all it's made out to be). But along the way you'll realize that you matter to God and that your existence impacts others, and you will no longer reside in the broken places, because you've found something much richer.

This is no less a miracle than the person who is healed instantly.

So, my friend, let's do this. Let's begin to soak in the truth that Jesus started your healing long ago, when He proclaimed His mission with you on His heart. The first step in this process is to establish a solid foundation—to understand what you *don't* have to do, because it's already been put in place just for you by Jesus.

Note
1. Jon Courson, "A Most Magnificent Mission—Luke 4:18-19," Sermon Index. net. http://www.sermonindex.net/modules/articles/index.php?view=article&aid=24495 (accessed October 2013).

1

What You Don't Have to Do

When the Greeks looked at a building's blueprint, they pictured the building whole and complete. . . . The Hebrews looked at the same blueprint more practically. They envisioned the process of building from hard hats to hammers, from scaffolding to skylights. "Ah," the Hebrews said. "This is perfect." The Hebrews and the early Christians understood perfection as a process, not a product.

KENDA CREASY DEAN, *THE GODBEARING LIFE*

"Do A and B, and C will happen."

"Stay on track."

"Try harder!"

"Pull yourself up by your bootstraps."

"What's wrong with you?!"

Have you heard any of these? Maybe you've even said them to yourself as you tried a hundred times and failed. Sheer willpower may have worked for a while. . . and then unraveled. Perhaps you look like you've got it all together, but the mess that is underneath is still there.

The reality is that most of us care very much about our well-being; so when people tell us to clean up our act and do better, it's just a rehash of promises we've made to ourselves, like:

I will try harder.
I will get past this somehow.
I...I...I...

Your list is more personalized because you know yourself like no other. But can we put our lists aside for a moment? There is power in choices, but let's begin by building a foundation on the choices we *don't* have to make.

THE JESUS FACTOR

Herod the king was distraught. A child had been born; his birth was heralded by the very angels (see Luke 2:13-14). Some said this baby was the Christ child, the long-awaited Messiah. Herod was a jealous man, so—even though he had absolute power and rule—in his insecurity he commanded a party of Magi (wise men in service to the king) to locate this child in order that his life might be taken. It is said that Jesus was born and weaned on the sounds of sorrow, for King Herod ordered the murder of every male child under the age of two in his attempt to do away with the Christ child. The news of this massacre could not have been held back from the ears of His parents, who had whisked Jesus away to safety. Scripture does not share what this young couple went through as they held their beloved child in their arms, keenly aware that others mourned with empty arms and shattered hearts because of their son.

It was a humble and tragic beginning to the earthly life and ministry of Jesus.

No wonder our heavenly Father looked down at the state of humanity and grieved. No wonder He sent His Son! This sorrowful entry underscored the theme of Christianity and the mission of Jesus: to save us from the grip sin had on humanity.

Do you want to know what else is tragic? When you are brokenhearted, the first instructions you are likely to receive are to do more, weep less, and be stronger.

But in reality, the most powerful act we can do is to rest in what He's already done for us. It's a foundation upon which all other change can be built.

Before you consider what you should be doing, or what you didn't do, or what you may need to do, let's fully explore what you don't have to do.

You Don't Have to Do This Alone

My two-year-old grandson, Luke, stands at the edge of the pool. He has on his floaties. An Elmo swim diaper. Sweet little yellow goggles that make him look like a frog. I stand waist-deep in water, my arms open wide.

"Come on, buddy. You can do this."

He edges closer and peers in, then backs away. After several trips back and forth, he finally sits on the edge of the pool and dips his toes in the water. I slip next to him when he's not looking and scoop him up and hold him close. Into the water we go.

"I got you, buddy," I whisper. "I got you."

He could fight me, but he trusts instead. After all, this is his Gaga. Over the next several minutes, Luke gains courage to go further and further, until finally he is jumping into my open arms. Any time he feels frightened, he whispers these words under his breath: "I got you, buddy. I got you."

It is his assurance that no matter how scary things might feel, he is not alone.

The reality is that sometimes we sense God calling us into deeper waters as part of our healing process, but we find the prospect intimidating. We aren't sure how to take the next step, or what to do if we take a dive and sink to the bottom. We want to trust, but it's downright scary.

The disciples felt that way too. In John 16:17-18, we see them congregating in a huddle to dissect something Jesus had just told them.

"In a little while you will see me no more," He had said (v. 16).

This news stirred anxiety in the hearts of the disciples. Up until this time, whenever they'd had a question or needed assurance, they could ask Him directly. They were accustomed to standing back and watching Him work. They were key eyewitnesses to the power of Jesus. His words caused them to worry.

What will we do without Him?

Whom will we turn to when we feel weak or unable?

What if we can't accomplish what Jesus says we can?

What if no one else sees in me what He does?

These men were focused on their imperfections and their potential to stumble—or to fall short in a big way. They could recount the times they had failed Jesus and one another. To be honest, for some of them, it was a mystery why Jesus had even chosen them. They were prime examples of human frailty—not anything special, at least as far as their culture or peers might define the word.

Jesus saw that they were brimming with worry: "Are you asking one another what I meant when I said, 'In a little while you will see me no more'?" (John 16:19).

He gently assured them that even in the absence of His earthly presence, He would still be with them. Close as a whisper. They could ask for what they needed in His name, and they would receive it. He saw their insecurity, and then reminded them that His love and plan for them weren't dependent on their efforts or worthiness, but on the Power that resided within them.

"In this world you will have trouble," He said. "But take heart! I have overcome the world" (John 16:33).

He steered their worried thoughts away from what they couldn't do or hadn't done and toward Himself, offering peace in exchange for their anxiety.

I got you, buddy. I got you.

Perhaps worry has been an integral part of your thought process for a long time. You may have come to believe that healing has something to do with what you bring to the table. Maybe, like my grandson Luke, you fear that jumping into the depths is just too big of a leap. You've listened to advice, and you've tried to get over it or pretend like it's not a big deal, but none of that has worked. You've made choices and sacrifices so you can find healing, but you've been broken for so long that you wonder if God can do a miracle in you.

How does Scripture respond to these fretful thoughts?

"Cast all your anxiety on him because he cares for you" (1 Pet. 5:7).

I got you, sis. I got you.

Jesus' message to His disciples, and to you and me, is that it's not our strength or power that will transform us. Yes, we make changes. Yes, we open our scabbed and broken heart to His tender touch. Yes, we allow Him to move us in uncomfortable directions to discover new paths—and leave old ones behind. But we can stop stressing, because our healing is not solely—or even primarily—dependent on us.

It's a partnership.

You and God—and He's bigger.

Perhaps you've come close to taking a leap of trust, but at the last moment you backed away. Maybe you've even dipped your toes in, thinking maybe that was enough. God isn't unaware of your fears or your failed attempts. He knows how scary this is for you. But He's asking you to allow Him to scoop you up and take you deeper, because there are things He sees that you don't yet. There are qualities He desires to instill in you that you aren't even aware of yet. There are elements of your faith, as you move from the edge of uncertainty to trust, that you have yet to explore.

Not too long ago, I stood in the pool again. Luke wore his floaties. He had on his Elmo swim diaper. His cute yellow goggles made him look like a little frog.

I held open my arms, and my two-year-old grandson jumped with glee into my arms. No reservations. No fear. This time I didn't have to say it, because it was ingrained on his heart:

I got you, buddy. I got you.

As you begin to heal, your God is with you every step of the way. You are not alone, and you don't have to do the work of healing alone.

Let's look at the next thing you *don't* have to do.

You Don't Have to Earn God's Love

> For God so loved the world that he gave his one and only Son, that whoever believes in him shall not perish but have eternal life. For God did not send his Son into the world to condemn the world, but to save the world through him (John 3:16-17).

This passage is the most familiar Scripture of the Christian faith. In fact, it's so familiar that the power contained within it can get lost.

God so loved the world.

Not just a little section of the world or one person over another. He chose from the beginning of creation to love all of us.

Sometimes believers try to compartmentalize this love, saying that God loves just those who look like them, or sound like them. That you have to be a certain way or live up to a certain standard before God loves you. But that's not how it works.

When I was a teenager newly in love with Jesus, John 3:16 was the first verse I memorized. However, it took years for its truth to be engraved on my identity as a child of God. Though I loved Jesus with my entire being, the belief that exterior accomplishments or merits represented my worth infiltrated my sense of who I was. Perhaps my value was based on how well I performed according to certain standards, or on whether I attended church often enough, read my Bible enough, or stepped into my full potential.

While all of these are good things to do, basing our identity on them is contradictory to the teachings of Christ, who described faith as being in a personal relationship with Him. In fact, He said that loving God was the greatest commandment (see Matt. 22:34-38). Years ago, a friend helped me climb out of the religious pit that kept me striving to earn God's love. He said, "Take your finger and draw an X in the air."

I felt silly, but I drew a large imaginary X between us.

"That's sin," my friend said. "It's what separates us from the destiny and heart of God. Good people with a heart to serve God—like the Pharisees, and later churches and denominations— built walls around that X in the form of a set of rules that they hoped would keep sin safely at a distance. When the next generation came along, they identified the wall of rules as sin, so they did the same. This created a maze of walls erected generation after generation, until the actual definition of sin became very murky."

It's no wonder Jesus quoted the words of Isaiah 61:1-2 when He stood in the temple that day.

By focusing on the question "Who are you, Jesus?" rather than talking about what the people should or shouldn't do, what they hadn't done, or what they could do, He demolished the murky definition of faith as He shared a very clear mission statement that pointed directly at Himself:

I've come to open the eyes of the blind.

I've come to set the prisoner free.

I've come with good news for the poor in spirit.

I've come to heal the brokenhearted.

I've come to break the chains of the oppressed.

No matter how you arrived at your brokenness, the power of the Cross is not found in what you do, but in what has already been done for you. This is not to say that you do not play a part. Jesus said, "I demand that you love each other as much as I love you" (John 15:12, *TLB*). Our role is to accept His love, and then to allow that love to lead us to love others. It's a grace-drenched existence wrapped around relationship.

A small tattoo on my wrist in Hebrew script spells out "grace." It is a visual reminder to me that, because of His sacrifice, there are no walls between me and God.

Any time I start to believe that I'm not enough, that I've fallen short, and that I'm not worthy of His love—or if I fall into the trap of trying to out-earn my Savior—this message shifts my focus from me to Him. It's a reminder that it's not my offerings that delight God, but my joyful acceptance of His love that brings Him pleasure (see Hos. 6:6).

A. W. Tozer put it this way: "What I am anxious to see in Christian believers is a beautiful paradox. I want to see in them the joy of finding God while at the same time they are blessedly pursuing Him. I want to see in them the great joy of having God yet always wanting Him."

Maybe you are struggling with this message right now because of the giant X with all the walls around it that has been your theological foundation. Well, I have great news for you.

The simple gospel message of God's love will not leave you unchanged. For when you return that love and begin to trust Jesus from the heart, you learn to listen for His voice. You sense when He is teaching you or redirecting you. You become fiercely aware of temptation—and when you feel the desire to give in or to allow idols of any kind to rise in stature in your life, you weigh those temptations in light of your love for your heavenly Father. This relationship without the maze of walls helps you discover your "true selves, [your] child-of-God selves" (John 1:12, *THE MESSAGE*).

You Don't Have to Run Anymore

As a young girl, I went to the crowded state fair with my mother. A neighbor family joined us; altogether there were eight children under the age of 10. The chance of losing a child along the way was high! My mother instructed me (I was a dreamer, and the most likely to get sidetracked and lost): "Suzie, if you get separated from the group, don't go down a different fairway or run in a different direction. Just stop and wait for me. I'll backtrack and find you. Just stay put."

When you have experienced brokenness, you may feel that you've taken a wrong turn somewhere. Perhaps that sense of lostness has sent you down paths you regret. It may have caused you to lie awake at night while frenzied thoughts raced through your mind. You can rest now. Let Jesus take you by the hand. You can get off that wandering side road you took in search of something or someone who could possibly make you feel less pain. You can slow down the activity that tells the world you've got it all together, though your heart hurts so much that you can't sleep at night.

Stop.

Right where you are.

You are found by Him.

One of the key truths we often ignore in our faith is that Jesus meets us where we are. A demoniac rushes from a dark and bleak cemetery, desperate for help. He is bound in chains and frightening to himself and to others (see Mark 5:1-20).

Jesus meets him right where he is.

A religious man named Nicodemus seeks Jesus under the cover of darkness. He is highly respected in his community, but his fears drive him to meet with Jesus in secret (see John 3:1-21).

Jesus meets him right where he is.

A woman kneels and pours perfume over Jesus' feet, while others look on with disdain (see Luke 7:36-50).

Jesus meets her right where she is.

Through each of these interactions, a life is changed. One walks away in "his right mind." Another becomes a courageous follower in broad daylight. Another realizes for the first time what it is like to be truly loved.

The more you understand Jesus' mission statement and recognize that it is for you, the more you are free to simply sit in His presence, expectant that the person you always knew lived inside of you will emerge with His touch. This is when the miracle begins to take place. You understand that He's "got you," that you are not alone, that you are loved, and that you can stop running.

THEN YOU TAKE HEART

Let's go back to John 16:33. The anxious disciples were worried that they couldn't do what they needed to do on their own.

Jesus told them, "In this world you will have trouble. But take heart! I have overcome the world."

Take heart.

Let's pause for a moment to receive courage and comfort from a few facts. First, let's recognize how strong you are.

Oh, Suzie, I'm not strong at all.

> **Take heart:** to receive courage or comfort from some fact

Aren't you? After all, you got up this morning, even though you may not have felt like it. You are seeking answers for yourself, and for those you care about. Each of these actions is a tribute to the truth that you desire nothing less than God's best. You are aware of your fragile places, but that's when the Jesus factor kicks in. You receive courage, for "when we are weak in ourselves, then we are strong in the grace of our Lord Jesus Christ" (see 2 Cor. 12:9).

A foundation of healing is built on the promise that God will be your strength. He is in the midst of this healing process with you—right where you are.

With all your baggage.

With your broken heart.

With your messy emotions.

With your faith and love for Him, in spite of the pain that just won't go away.

All that is required of you is to accept what He so willingly offers.

Even if these are concepts you've heard your whole life, you may still be saying, "Can it really be so simple?"

The truth is that many of us, even though we can quote Scripture and unearth the Hebrew and Greek meanings of words and phrases, are still striving. We are so focused on what we haven't done or what we need to do or the broken pieces that seem too fragmented to put back together that we've forgotten the power of what Jesus offers. We can be immersed in Christian culture and forget what He has done.

But there's good news. When we rediscover what Jesus offers, we join in with the multitudes of others who sing:

My chains fell off, my heart was free; I rose, went forth, and followed Thee.[1]

LET'S START PEELING AWAY THOSE LAYERS

A scene from one of my favorite movies, *Shrek*, offers some helpful insight into the way our perceptions and understanding of life change during the healing process. Donkey and Shrek are walking along together.

Shrek says, "For your information, there's a lot more to ogres than people think."

Donkey says, "Example?"

"Example . . . uh . . . ogres are like onions!" Shrek holds up an onion, which Donkey sniffs.

Donkey isn't getting it, and he guesses three or four ways that Shrek could be like an onion. As Shrek starts to peel the onion, he says, "Layers. Onions have layers. Ogres have layers. Onions have layers. You get it? We both have layers."[2]

Shrek was telling Donkey that there's more to a person than what can be seen on the surface. When you are in pursuit of a mended heart, the Holy Spirit will gently peel away one layer of brokenness at a time. It's a merciful and exquisite process that gradually reveals the healed and whole person you are meant to be.

As we dig into this process together, I invite you to make it personal, taking time to interact with God about the work He may want to do in each layer of your heart.

Even if some chapters don't seem to apply to you, the underlying precept might. Maybe your husband didn't leave you (like

Carol's in the next chapter), but you understand abandonment. Perhaps you haven't lost a loved one (like Amber in chapter 4), but you know what it is to mourn what you cannot bring back. In each chapter, there will be those "a-ha!" moments when the Holy Spirit speaks just to you. Rather than try to write about every life event that can bring brokenness, my hope was to connect with the underlying need and then explore how Jesus' mission statement meets that need.

As you go through this study, write in your journal. Underline in this book. Scribble your thoughts in the margins. Don't be afraid to go deeper as the Holy Spirit leads. If a moment is painful, pause and let the pain be exposed long enough to sense Jesus' touch in the midst of it.

As you respond to the questions in the "Just You and God" sections, be assured that there are no right answers. This is intended to be a time of simple intimacy with your heavenly Father as, one by one, layers are gently lifted and peeled away, and you discover together what is underneath.

JUST *You* AND *God*

1. Read John 4:10 and Matthew 18:12-14. What is God saying to you through these verses?

2. What is the difference between focusing on your choices and accepting *His* choices made on your behalf?

3. Read John 9:25 and Luke 19:1-8. What happened when each of these individuals encountered Jesus?

_____

_____

_____

4. Write down Luke 4:18, but put your name in this Scripture. Place this personalized verse in a place where you will see it every day this week.

_____

_____

_____

5. Read Galatians 5:1. "Work-harder" teachings are a "yoke of slavery" like the one described in this verse. What does Jesus offer in place of this burden?

_____

_____

_____

6. One of the promises in Jesus' mission statement is that He brings "good news." After reading today's chapter, the good news for you is . . . (finish the sentence in your own words).

_____

_____

_____

7. In this chapter, you read about three things you don't have to do. In fact, the more you *don't* do these things, the more you live in Him. The more you *don't* do these things, the more you build a foundation of rest. The more you *don't*

do these things, the more joy you rediscover in your faith. Describe your response to this:

_____

_____

_____

THE MENDED HEART PRINCIPLE #1:
TAKE HEART

The power of the Cross is not in what you do,
but in what has already been done for you.

PRAYER

Dear Jesus, You came to heal me! I freely step onto the solid foundation already built by You. I stop right where I am and lift my arms up to You. I embrace and accept Your gifts fully as I take heart in You.

MENDED HEART CHALLENGE

- Write down the three things you don't have to do.
- Read that list daily.
- If you start to strive or hide or think you're all alone, make a choice to rest in what God has done for you.

Notes

1. Charles Wesley, "And Can It Be That I Should Gain?" quoted in Stephen F. Olford with David L. Olford, *Anointed Expository Preaching* (Nashville, TN: Broadman & Holman Publishers, 1998), p. 224.
2. From the movie *Shrek*, DreamWorks Animation, 2001. http://www.imdb.com/character/ch0002002/quotes (accessed October 2013).

PART 2

Hearts in the Midst of Mending

2

When People Hurt Your Heart

Focus on giants—you stumble. Focus on God—your giants tumble.

MAX LUCADO, *CAST OF CHARACTERS*

Carol flipped open her phone to read a text message from her husband. Little did she know, her life was getting ready to fall apart. *I've taken all my things and I won't be back. I'm done,* the message read. In that moment, Carol drew her first breath as a single woman and mom.

The days that followed were filled with questions:

What now?

Why did he do this to me?

Is there hope for our marriage?

Where are You, God?

The choices of her husband seemed to reinforce the message she had heard her whole life: "You aren't really wanted." Carol felt dinged and dented, and her future was uncertain. The words that flew back and forth between her and her husband were spoken from pain and were often meant to cut—and they did. There were moments when Carol had to remind herself to breathe, because she felt paralyzed by fear.

Piled on top of fear were regret and shame stemming from the word "divorced." The only thing that brought Carol joy was holding close her 20-month-old daughter, who had no idea of the lives that were crumbling around her.

Carol and her husband were involved in their community. He was on staff at their church. She was in full-time ministry.

How did we get here from there? Carol often wondered.

The shattered pieces of her marriage seemed to be on display for the whole world to judge, and the faith that she claimed was tested. She often stood in the doorway of her baby's room, where the most valuable gift she had received through her marriage resided. She focused on her child and talked herself into surviving one more day, reasoning that there must be a purpose for doing so. Her little girl was worth fighting for.

Except for her daughter, Carol began to isolate herself from other people. She had convinced herself that if no one could get to her, she would never be hurt again. But as time passed, Carol began to long for more. This desire started with seemingly insignificant moments, such as a sweet smile from someone she didn't know, or the thoughtfulness of a stranger who held an umbrella for her as she wrestled with a stroller in the grocery parking lot.

These small kindnesses seemed to be whispers that God was there. They also forced Carol to smile back and say thank you because, after all, that's what a Southern girl did.

Her hunger for more caused her to look for God in ways she had only talked about before her husband left. According to Carol, her faith had been an "always there" accessory, but now it was what helped her exist moment by moment. She struggled financially for the first time. She was working as hard as she could, but the money just didn't stretch far enough. Diapers showed up from friends and strangers, even though she was too proud to ask. Her daycare needs were met when it seemed impossible to do it alone. Each day, she turned more to the God she professed faith in and the promises she had learned since childhood. But even as she was making it, Carol still wondered if the pain would ever subside. She had read about healing in the Bible, but she didn't know if it was for her. She didn't have leprosy or a withered hand. There was no debilitating disease from which she needed to be cured.

In fact, no one could see how serious her heart condition was from the outside. She could play the part and say all the right words. She could be funny and brave and strong—except for when the lights were low and no one was watching.

When Carol looks back on that season of her life, she believes that God carried her during those first few months. Though she woke up each day with a hurting heart, something greater was sustaining her and protecting her.

WE CAN LOSE HEART
BECAUSE OF PEOPLE

In *The Mom I Want to Be*, I referenced a story that took place over 20 years ago at a Turning Point conference. At that time I was working with teens, and my church sent me as a conferee. The facilitator flipped the lights off and a film started playing.

The movie was about a dysfunctional family in the midst of a meltdown moment. Mom and Dad were arguing. One child was screaming in defiance. Another hid around the corner in angst. Then I saw her. She was the peacemaker. Trying to make everything okay. Like a tightrope walker, she asked the screaming teen to stop yelling as she attempted to comfort her little brother. She was trying to keep the pieces from falling all around her, but she simply wasn't old or wise or big enough.

I heard someone crying nearby, and I was filled with compassion for whoever was sobbing.

Wow, that person must have been really hurt in the past to cry so publicly. Why isn't anyone helping her?

Then I realized that the sobbing person was me. I jumped up out of my seat, left the room, and found an empty stall in the women's bathroom. I crawled up on the toilet seat and huddled, trying to stop the tears that seemed to have no end.

A pair of red shoes appeared, just visible under the door of the stall.

"Can I come in?" a woman's voice asked.

"No," I replied. "You can't."

"Are you okay?"

"I've been okay for a long time," I whispered. "I don't understand this. I'm here because I want to help others. This is crazy."

The red shoes remained still for a few seconds, and then I heard these words: "Honey, sometimes God lets you remember for a reason."

The sight of that little peacemaker in the movie had triggered emotions long healed. Perhaps that is the most powerful lesson I took away from that conference, and it's one I still hold close today. We can become so whole (a wonderful gift!) that we forget the magnitude of what we have been given. God reached down to give me a glimpse into the brokenness I had once carried as a little peacemaker, and to remind me how much He had healed my shattered heart.

It had been a long time since I had felt such pain. It was heavy. It made me sad. It went deep into my being.

Many of us carry that weight of sadness as a result of the people factor in our lives. It may be our childhood, an ex, a parent or an in-law who inflicts the pain. The people factor impacts those who are rich, those who are poor, those who are married and those who are not. It reaches to the addicted, the hardened and the innocent. Whatever the specifics of the situation, the common thread is a desire to be free of that hurtful influence—not necessarily removed from the person, but healed of the pain associated with the relationship.

At another conference—one at which I was speaking—I mentioned my children-in-law and the blessing they were to us. Afterwards, many young moms privately sought me out, sharing how they longed to hear those same words from a mother-in-law, or how they had married their husbands only to discover that their new families played havoc on their relationships or sense of self.

Whenever or however it took place, when you've been hurt by the people factor, you just want to be whole and discover what God has for you—regardless of what another person has done.

What is the people factor in your broken places?

Are the people who once hurt you still calling the shots in your emotions or in the way you view yourself? Is an old wound damaging current relationships? Perhaps your offender has been out of your life for years, or is even deceased, but their actions or words continue to impact:

- How you interact with others
- Your identity
- Emotions that linger or rise up at the worst times
- Attitudes or behaviors that lead to unhealthy responses, such as enablement, people pleasing, consuming caretaking, striving, overcontrol, mistrust, lashing out, withdrawal, and more

If you are struggling with any of these symptoms, you may feel marked or branded or unloved or unworthy. You probably find yourself asking, "When will they release their hold on my life?"

THE JESUS FACTOR

Former friends plotted together in secret places and in hidden meetings, hoping for the apostle Paul's arrest—even his death. Scripture describes times when Paul was utterly discouraged. But he had a secret that he longed to share:

> Remember, our Message is not about ourselves; we're proclaiming Jesus Christ, the Master. All we are is messengers, errand runners from Jesus for you. It started when God said, "Light up the darkness!" and our lives filled up with light as we saw and understood God in the face of Christ, all bright and beautiful.
>
> If you only look at us, you might well miss the brightness. We carry this precious Message around in the unadorned clay pots of our ordinary lives (2 Cor. 4:5-7, *THE MESSAGE*).

A jar of clay is common. If it breaks or is chipped, it's not as significant a loss as it would be if a beautiful bowl or vase or lamp made of precious metals and jewels were broken. Unless, of course, there's something special about that ordinary, damaged vessel that isn't visible at first glance.

Paul was an ordinary man. His secret was that a Light blazed within him, shining through the cracks of his brokenness. This Light lit the way for others to follow as it filled the once-dark places that lingered in his heart. It revealed the glory of Christ in the midst of wretched humanity, and offered something of such great substance to Paul and those who ministered alongside him that they were "hard pressed on every side, but not crushed; perplexed, but not in despair; persecuted, but not abandoned; struck down, but not destroyed" (2 Cor. 4:8-9).

I don't know about you, but to me, being hard pressed, perplexed, persecuted and struck down sounds like a pretty bad day.

> **kardia** [Greek] translated heart: the heart; mind, character, inner self, will, intention, center; the central or innermost part; the essential or most vital part of something.

But this Light helped Paul not to lose heart. Regardless of what other people did or didn't do, the central or innermost part of his being remained unaffected. In fact, it blazed even brighter: "Therefore we do not lose heart. Though outwardly we are wasting away, yet inwardly we are being renewed day by day. For our light and momentary troubles are achieving for us an eternal glory that far outweighs them all" (vv. 16-17).

Paul understood all too well how much it hurts when a person rejects you, abandons you, says hurtful words, or simply doesn't have what it takes to love you in the right ways. It's interesting that he called his troubles light and momentary, because by most standards they were anything but.

People who had once called out his name in praise and threw their cloaks at his feet in honor (see Acts 7:58–8:1a) now plotted to take his life. He had been beaten, shipwrecked, imprisoned, hunted down and betrayed. He suffered loneliness, rejection and abandonment.

How in the world could any of this be described as momentary and light?

It was because Paul gave less weight to people than to the Messiah who lived inside of him.

FREED FROM
THE EFFECTS OF SIN

Jesus had liberated Paul from a life of sin years earlier, and that same gift also offered power to overcome the *effects* of the sins of people upon Paul's life (see Eph. 1:19-21).

Let's let that soak in for a moment. Yes, Jesus took our sins upon Him at the cross, but it doesn't stop there. That same act frees us from the effects of the sins of others upon our own heart.

That's the Jesus factor! We can live free from the inside out, regardless of what people have done to our exterior. John El-dredge, in *Waking the Dead*, writes:

> You get the picture. [Paul's] life has been hard. It has been war. His vita reads something like out of Amnesty International. Somebody has been trying to shut him up or shut him down. He knows something; he has a secret to tell. So, how, Paul—*how*? How do we not lose heart? *So we fix our eyes not on what is seen, but on what is unseen (2 Cor. 4:18)*. . . . This wise old seer is saying that there is a way of looking at life, and that those who discover it are able to live from the heart no matter what.[1]

PEOPLE LOSE POWER

Our heart mends as our inner self—the central or innermost part of our identity—is wrapped around the Light inside of us, rather than around the people who have harmed us. This one small step changes the way we see things. We begin to differentiate between people and God.

This means that the words that were spoken over your life, the things that happened to you, the evil you endured, or the love gap that you feel—these are not your legacy anymore.

People may have hammered at your fragile clay exterior. They may have even chipped a few pieces away, or caused cracks that run deep. But inside of you is a bright, glorious Light—and because of that, it's not what is seen or felt or experienced that defines you. You are no longer hemmed in by human limitations stemming from flawed thinking:

- When she changes, I'll change.
- If only he would love me more, then I'd be okay.
- If that person hadn't hurt me, I'd be happy.
- Because of what he/she did, I have every reason to feel this way.

Each of these approaches involves waiting for someone else to change, to fill you up, or to say they are sorry. Hoping that one person will give you what someone else didn't. Looking for affirmation in other people or in the things you do. Hoping that your dad (or mom or husband or friend) will say those words that let you know your value. Hoping that something or someone on the exterior will heal you.

But what if that other person doesn't change? What if he or she doesn't hold back those unkind words? What if an offender is no longer in the picture, or your pain isn't their priority? Real transformation begins as we place people in the proper framework of our healing.

In *The Mom Factor*, Dr. Henry Cloud and Dr. John Townsend state that it is our responsibility to grieve and forgive what we did not receive from people in the past so that we can be healed. This takes place as we open our hearts to receive what we did not get.[2]

I have friends who were raised by an alcoholic parent(s). Their stories vary, but the pain does not. Some had a parent who was up and down—one moment laughing, the next angry. For most of these friends, their childhood homes were emotional roller coasters. Many of them became caregivers. They answered the phone and told lies to cover the fact that their parent was in the next room, blacked out, or that they had found him or her sleeping on the front porch that morning after an all-nighter and had helped them change their clothes and had put them to bed.

Many of these friends have recounted conversations held under the influence of alcohol. One friend described her mother's suicidal threats, and how she struggled with both the fear and the hope that she would "just do it." Another remembers vile and hurtful words, and how her mother remembered none of it the next day. If my friend tried to discuss it, she was expected to just forget it, for how could those words be held against her mom if there was no inkling of it in her memory?

When you have been affected by a parent who is an alcoholic (or neglectful or absent or disengaged or abusive), it can make you long so badly for a healthy parent that you feel pathetic. You aren't pathetic, of course, for the desire to bond with a parent arises within the human heart from the moment a child enters this world. It's a common human need. Because of this need, you might make it your job to fix your parent(s) to increase your odds. Or you confuse forgiving with taking abuse, and everything gets muddled, to the point that you both love and hate your parent(s). You pour out or hide their alcohol, take your punishment when you are found out, and pray for the day when your home life looks like the person's down the street. Or you push against the abuse, all the while holding out hope that things will get better.

When none of this works, it leaves a bigger void.

Which leads to trying to fill that void. Some experiment with drugs or alcohol in their teens or later years. (The philosophy is that if you can't beat them, you might as well join them.) Others take a road as far away from their parent's path as they can and try to fill their lives with good things, like hard work or achieving success or being perfect in every area.

But long after you've grown up, and even as you live a stable life, the people factor can keep you in a vulnerable place.

You observe others interacting with their families. You see a healthy and supportive mother or mother-in-law with one of your friends or a neighbor, while you're taking care of your baby and tending your parent's emotional needs. You see dads who say kind things about their daughters, while your dad's words and actions (or lack thereof) cut deep.

The people factor has failed you.

What do you do? You can remain in the cycle of asking someone who is not capable of doing it to fill that void, or you can find what you need in a different place. One friend, who wishes to remain anonymous because of her mother's continued addiction, says:

> When I stopped looking for my mom to meet my needs, it helped me to see that she had never had her needs met either. My mom looked for help in a bottle, and the temptation was for me to follow. But Christ is my need-meeter. And when I began to look to Him to fill me up, I found that I could love my mom, and with some healthy boundaries have a relationship with her. But I was changed. I stopped demanding spiritually and emotionally and physically that she give me something she couldn't give. I filled up with my Savior, and it absolutely released me.

When we stop asking people to be our need-meeters, we discover Paul's secret for ourselves. People, whether through evil or selfishness or simply their own brokenness, can harm us, but that doesn't limit who we can be or what God can do in us. Even when people don't change, or they fail to do what they should, or our best efforts to help them blow up in our faces, our value and worth and identity aren't based on how they treat us. They may refuse to change, but that decision doesn't stop us from growing and changing—and finding fulfillment in Christ.

As you release the people factor to hold close the Jesus factor—as you stop looking to mere humans to make you feel valued or worthwhile—you become free to place people in God's hands as you find the love you have always desired. You are also free to reach out to healthy friends and mentors who can speak into your life. You can hear the words "I'm proud of you" from those individuals and accept the affirmation without looking over your shoulder, hoping to hear the same words from an addicted or broken parent or other person.

If you have been impacted by the people factor, as I once was, you are no longer just a child of a broken adult(s) or a broken person; you are a strong, talented, interesting child of God who wants better for yourself and those you care about. When you look to Jesus instead of people, you are able to be honest about the flawed people factor (it is what it is) while allowing the Jesus factor to show you how to give grace where it's needed. You receive the wisdom to know what you can control and what you can't. You learn to set boundaries when people's intentions are harmful or their actions destructive.

Most importantly, the Jesus factor allows you to look at your own heart to see where God desires to effect change. You stop basing your wellness on whether someone else is changing, or on the pace at which they are dealing with their broken places.

The Jesus factor breaks the ties that bind us to another human being.

Scripture tells us, "Humans can reproduce only human life, but the Holy Spirit gives birth to spiritual life" (John 3:6, *NLT*).

This understanding realigns your identity from what mankind did to who God is and who you are to Him. Your heart and belief system will be fundamentally rewired as you start to give priority to these truths:

- No person is greater than your God (see 1 John 4:4).
- Your heavenly Father loves you unconditionally (see 1 John 3:1).
- Nothing can ever separate you from His love (see Rom. 8:38-39).
- Your name is written on the palm of His hand (see Isa. 49:16).
- Regardless of another person's actions, you are marked with destiny (see 1 Cor. 2:9).

Therefore, Don't Lose Heart

To lose heart: to lose one's courage or confidence

Is Jesus aware of Carol's or my friends' or your broken places caused by the people factor? Maybe that's a question you've wrestled with. To answer it, I could try to write a profound and deeply theological explanation of how God uses pain to teach us, or how our trials produce righteousness. Instead, I'll tell you the simple truth.

Yes, He is aware.

In Jeremiah 8:21, God speaks through a young prophet, saying, "I hurt with the hurt of my people. I mourn and am overcome with grief" (*NLT*). In the next chapter, we see God weeping over the actions of an entire nation, saying, "Oh, that my head were a spring of water and my eyes a fountain of tears!" (Jer. 9:1). Through this passage and many others, we find not only that God is aware of the pain that people endure at the hands of others, but also that this grief was on His heart the day He sent Jesus to earth, with humanity—including me and you—fixed firmly in His sights.

God has never been an advocate of sin or its effect upon His beloved.

In Carol's case, it was not His will that a marriage be destroyed by unfaithfulness or abandonment. His Word directs spouses to honor each other—to love as Christ loved the Church, with a pure and sacrificial love (see Eph. 5:25).

Nor is it God's intention for children to be neglected or abused in any way by a parent. It was Jesus who called out to the little children to crawl up on His lap rather than be ignored or overlooked (see Matt. 19:14).

In hindsight, I know that He saw that little peacemaker who hid her baby brother in the closet when things seemed out of control.

He was with me when I ran away at the age of 13—and walked back in the pelting rain because I had no place to go.

He was not far away when I was a rebellious teenager, and He was a constant shadow when I was alone in a big city at the age of 17.

He was present when I stood in a small church and reached out for His love. He was there when I held my newborn in my arms for the first time, and as I prayed that God would change the next generation through me.

Our Savior grieves with us over the people factor; at the same time, He longs to partner with us as we enter a new chapter in our lives. With the human factor alone, we can overcome a great deal. Through sheer determination and effort, we can climb over obstacles to stand stronger. But when we shift our identity from our relationship with a broken person to a God who loves us, who has always loved us, and who is deeply burdened over the sin of mankind and its effect upon His beloved children, that partnership leads to the Light Paul described earlier:

> But we have this treasure in jars of clay to show that this all-surpassing power is from God and not from us. We are hard pressed on every side, but *not* crushed; perplexed, but *not* in despair; persecuted, but *not* abandoned; struck down, but *not* destroyed (2 Cor. 4:7-9, emphasis added).

It's the *not*s of that verse that lead to your mended heart. People become secondary to the love and plan that God speaks over you.

YOU BECOME A BEAUTIFUL, CRACKED CLAY POT

My friend Carol would love it that I'm calling her a crackpot. She's a funny mess, and delightfully deep in her faith. She is absolutely a beautiful, cracked clay pot. It's now been several years since Carol's divorce. She says:

> I may be hurt again. But I have come to know that God cuts such a profound path through my pain, that the dark times I walked through have given me an even deeper understanding of who He is and the way He loves me.

She still sees herself as broken, but she no longer feels like her life has been shattered. Rather, she is like a mosaic with a Light shining from the inside out. In fact, when she shares her testimony, she holds up a clay pot, broken and glued back together, for the audience to see. It's not perfect—or even beautiful by most human standards—but the Light filtering through the cracks is.

What does God want to do inside of you as you take the focus off of people and allow His Light to illuminate the cracks and chips of your life? Take a moment and point to where the breaking took place, and how, but then hold your cracked pot up to Him. What beautiful patterns are flickering in the dissipating shadows?

JUST *You* AND *God*

1. How have your interactions with hurtful people affected the way you see God, or the way you think He sees you?

   _____

   _____

   _____

2. In light of John 3:6, describe how a distorted image of God can keep you stuck.

   _____

   _____

   _____

3. Focusing on the Jesus factor instead of people will change: (1) the way you think; (2) the way you relate to people; and/ or (3) the way you see yourself. Which of these do you sense the Holy Spirit leading you to alter with God's help?

   _____

   _____

   _____

4. Write down the name of one person who has caused you pain. Are you willing to offer up your feelings about that person to Him today? Make it a prayer.

_____

_____

_____

_____

5. Paul described his troubles with people as momentary and light, even though he had been hurt deeply by people. How did he live in the nots of 2 Corinthians 4:8? What does his example show you?

_____

_____

_____

_____

6. Read Ephesians 1:18-20. What was the heart of Paul's prayer? What is the truth he wanted his readers to grasp?

_____

_____

_____

_____

7. When you held up the dings, dents, cracks and chips, did you note how they took place? Where and when they happened? Who was involved? Now, let's look at the Light within. Let that Light shine fully through the cracks. How does that change what you see?

_____

_____

_____

_____

THE MENDED HEART PRINCIPLE #2:
DON'T LOSE HEART

The Jesus factor is greater than the people factor.

PRAYER

Dear Jesus, I open every door to the place where people have hurt me. Shine Your Light and let Your work begin. Today I will shift my focus to You rather than dwelling on people or the past. Thank You for filling my gaps to overflowing with You.

MENDED HEART CHALLENGE

- Consider how much thought and energy you devote on a daily basis to thinking about people who have caused you pain.
- Prayerfully ask God to help you shift that focus.
- Praise God that He willingly took sin (even the effects of others' sins) from you.

Notes
1. John Eldredge, *Waking the Dead* (Nashville, TN: Thomas Nelson, 2003), pp. 22-23.
2. Dr. Henry Cloud and Dr. John Townsend, *The Mom Factor* (Grand Rapids, MI: Zondervan, 1996), p. 21.

3

When the Church Hurts Your Heart

*Your life is also part of a larger movement, a mystical fellowship,
the Kingdom of God advancing here on earth. That fellowship of the
Ransom being Restored—that is an amazing fellowship to be a part of.
To be sure, it's messy. Have you noticed in Paul's letters to the young
church how often he has to intervene in relationships?*

STASI ELDREDGE, *CAPTIVATING*[1]

Religious abuse?

Those words knocked Amy off balance. *Is that a thing?*

Could it be that there were others? Enough of them for
there to actually be a category with a name for what she had
suffered? Amy was in her mid-twenties. When her therapist said
those words to her, it was the first time she had ever considered
the possibility. Over several weeks, Amy had painstakingly un-
folded her story in the counselor's office. The counselor spent
hours listening, asking questions, and taking copious notes in
order to get to the bottom of Amy's debilitating panic attacks
and anxiety. This was the first time the counselor had offered
anything in the way of feedback.

The possibility that her brokenness was a result of spiritual
abuse stunned Amy.

She longed to feel better. Despite the weekly counseling sessions and medication, her life felt out of control. She was confused by her behavior; it wasn't unusual for her to drink until she blacked out, and sometimes she woke up in a strange bed next to a man she didn't know well.

She hated her choices—and at times hated herself—but only ended up doing the same things over and over again.

As she had shared the story of her childhood with the counselor, one central character emerged: her father. He was a pastor when Amy was growing up—and he was full of rage. Most of the people in the church didn't know that. No, the church people thought he was delightful. His smile and good-natured public persona belied the way he dealt with those close to him behind closed doors.

When Amy was 16, she wanted to go on a short-term missions trip. Her father disagreed with the location. Although her fear of him meant she rarely crossed him, this time Amy protested. She tried to explain that she felt God was calling her to this specific place. With a red face and veins bulging in his neck, her father backed Amy against a wall and screamed, "To you, and in this house, I AM GOD!" It was as if she had no feelings, thoughts or opinions.

As if she couldn't think for herself, much less hear from God.

Amy grew up in a home long on religion but short on grace—at least as far as her dad was concerned. Losing her voice and personal power was the costly price of her religious upbringing, and later she discovered that this was a primary source of the fear that plagued her life. That fear led to destructive behavior, for when a man wanted something from her, she didn't feel she could say no. She didn't feel entitled to assert her own wishes or boundaries.

Drinking and drugs became Amy's escape from her choices and the way they made her feel.[2]

WHY TALK ABOUT THIS?

I struggled with whether to include this type of brokenness in *The Mended Heart*. My desire is to build up the church and point others to it—not to criticize it or tear it down. Yet Jesus Himself often addressed the topic of religious abuse, and sadly you don't have to go far to hear how someone has been wounded by religion or individuals in a church.

Perhaps one of the most confusing questions of all time relates to how faith in God, such a rich and beautiful gift, can be used to harm and hold back those whom Jesus desires to reach. History shows us time and again how religion, in the hands of broken human beings, can fall far from the original intent.

What exactly is religious abuse?

It's the use of intimidation, guilt and fear to control and manipulate behavior in the name of God. And it can absolutely lead to spiritual brokenness. It distorts the way a person views God, or the way that person believes He sees him or her. It can lead a person away from faith, because the person feels that he or she can never earn a place in God's heart.

But Jesus says, "And I, when I am lifted up from the earth, will draw all people to myself" (John 12:32).

Oh, how spiritual abuse grieves our Savior's heart, as it's so opposite of what was intended on the cross! Maybe that's why Jesus spoke to the topic of spiritual abuse (and those who practiced it) so often.

It's why it's important that we talk about it, too.

THE JESUS FACTOR

When Jesus spoke His mission statement in that Nazareth synagogue, it was shortly after He returned from one of the most intense spiritual battles recorded in Scripture. His public ministry had launched weeks earlier with a grand display as God Himself declared from the heavens that this was indeed His Son (see Luke 3:22).

Then, rather than marching straight to a pulpit or establishing a church, Jesus followed the Holy Spirit into a lonely and bleak place for 40 days. There the enemy dangled temptations before Him, daring Him to demonstrate His power by producing bread from a rock or throwing Himself off a high cliff so that angels might save Him, and offering earthly reign if Jesus would only bow and worship him (see Luke 4:1-13).

We might underestimate the difficulty of this trial; after all, Jesus is the Son of God. But He was also fully human, and He experienced all that mankind might experience. He was hungry, exhausted and isolated—for 40 days. The biblical account paints this spiritual warfare as severe. Finally the enemy admitted defeat and slunk away, but Jesus didn't gain the victory by means of His physical prowess, or even by outwitting and outlasting Satan. Rather, He vanquished him with the simple and mighty sword of truth.

Jesus won the battle by consistently referring back to the One who had sent Him and to the written Word, as if to say:

I'm not here for a show of power.

I'm not here for my own selfish ends.

I'm not here to dazzle the world (or you) with my talent or supernatural abilities.

Instead, Jesus replied, "The Scriptures say, 'You must worship the LORD your God and serve only him'" (Luke 4:8). In this snapshot, we view the heart of true Christian leadership. It's the attitude of a servant who obeys the soft whisper of the Holy Spirit, even in the hardest of places, and who lives so that others might gain a glimpse of God's glory.

It's submissive, but not weak.

It speaks with authority, but in no way does it reflect a celebrity mindset, seeking fame or fawning.

In fact, if we were to sketch this leader, we would depict a dirty, hungry and unassuming warrior. Powerful in humility even when no human eyes are turned his way.

Stephen F. Olford, a twentieth-century Christian leader who positively influenced and trained many pastors, including Dr. Billy Graham, noted that Jesus walked into that battle filled with the Holy Spirit, and then walked out of the wilderness with a heart to reach those who were on God's heart. He says:

> There are five categories of people [the poor, the burdened or brokenhearted, the oppressed, the blind, and those who are in bondage or captivity] who must be reached redemptively, and this can never happen without the anointing. Indeed, more often than not, many preachers drive people away. This is a serious matter and demands careful thought and self-examination. Jesus always drew needy people to Himself: "The common people heard Him gladly" (Mark 12:37).[3]

In Amy's case, the gospel was overshadowed by a man who, instead of drawing his little girl to Christ, broke her heart and spirit. His authority was founded on his position as daddy, pastor and respected man of the cloth, but somehow, along the way, Jesus' mission was removed from the message, and a little girl all grown up got lost as well.

SPIRITUAL ABUSE IS AN OLD STORY

Jesus spent a great deal of time talking about (and to) the religious. They were the ones who received the boldest of instructions, encouragement and rebuke, whether He was speaking to His own disciples or to those who studied and taught the Law.

He spent most of His time hanging around synagogues, in homes, on mountaintops, in crowds, and in public places where the religious gathered. His insight and His words by turns inspired, convicted, astounded, confounded and angered His listeners.

God loves the sinner, but He also loves the church enough to call them from dark or unlovely places of thinking. One of Jesus' most painful encounters came when two sects (different groups who loved the same God but held differing beliefs) cornered Him to try to trick Him with questions. When they failed, Jesus turned to the crowd, saying:

> The scribes and the Pharisees have seated themselves in the chair of Moses; therefore all that they tell you, do and observe, but do not do according to their deeds; for they say things and do not do them. They tie up heavy burdens and lay them on men's shoulders, but they themselves are unwilling to move them with so much as a finger. But they do all their deeds to be noticed by men; for they broaden their phylacteries and lengthen the tassels of their garments. They love the place of honor at banquets and the chief seats in the synagogues, and respectful greetings in the market places, and being called Rabbi by men (Matt. 23:2-7, *NASB*).

This is a brave speech. These religious men held high positions of authority both in the church and over those who attended. That power reached beyond the church into the halls of government.

Of course, not all of the Pharisees and scribes (those entrusted to hand copy religious documents) were self-centered, pompous and dangerous. There were godly men among the Pharisees, Sadducees, Essenes and Zealots who wanted nothing more than to please God, who loved their families and others, and who followed their traditions out of a desire to honor the commandments and the Law.

Unfortunately, those who had succumbed to power—or who had been raised to lead or oversee, but without the beauty of knowing and serving God—overshadowed those who had not.

In the present day, it's not hard to see the far-reaching effects of religious power that has gotten out of balance. However, it's very hard to convince someone whose heart has been marked by it to return to faith. This is exactly what Amy experienced, and it was even more confusing for her because her father was a pastor and everyone looked up to him. After years of struggling, Amy came to believe that she was the problem. After all, she was constantly berated and told that she was rebellious. Often, her father warned her that her lack of obedience was going to cause her to spend eternity in hell. His insistence on legalistic perfection was based on parameters set by none other than himself. Though Amy had always known that her father was difficult to deal with, when she began to understand the depth of the damage he had inflicted on her heart, she was furious.

She went down the path of bitterness for a while, until she realized that it was only leading her further into heartbreak.

OUR VERY DIFFERENT EXPERIENCES

If you talk with a thousand people, you'll hear a thousand different stories of their experience with church. It's intriguing that, even within a specific congregation, one might describe the church as a positive, life-affirming experience, while another says it was damaging. As we look into the topic of spiritual abuse, it's not about criticizing or blaming a particular denomination or the Church as a whole, but about how we can recognize spiritual abuse and heal from it.

My story is the opposite of Amy's. When I became a Christian, I didn't know the story of Noah and the Ark. I had not been sprinkled, immersed, or baptized in any style. I hadn't attended kid's camp or Sunday School, though I did go to VBS (Vacation Bible School) on a bus when I was a child. When I became a Christian, the adults around me loved me in spite of my immaturity in the faith. They had no idea what was going on in my home at that time, and though as a teen I sometimes frustrated them, their consistent and faithful acts provided a sanctuary for me. I was drawn into Christianity by the presence of God and His Spirit, but I grew spiritually because of caring and well-meaning people.

I met Christians in that same church who didn't live out their faith well. I watched each week as one or two members of the youth group teased a girl each Sunday. This girl was frizzy-haired and not pretty in the high school sense, and sometimes she spoke without thinking. I thought she was brave, because she came back every week, even though she knew what was coming. Church was a safe place where God showed up, but also a place where you might or might not fit in.

The pastor of that church was a godly man. He talked about Jesus in a way that I could understand, and if I close my eyes, I can still picture him standing behind the pulpit with a guitar, singing, "Oh, How I Love Jesus."

Later, when two leaders in the church left their respective spouses and married each other, it split the church and fractured entire families. It broke that pastor's heart, for the church was never the same after that.

The whole thing was baffling to me. I had thought that my new church family would be less dysfunctional than my biological family, and they were. People opened their homes to me. They cared about me. They truly loved God. But they weren't *perfect*. Sometimes—most times—they were human, to a fault. If I were a true skeptic, I would look at my early introduction to faith and cite all the bad parts as reasons not to believe. Yet the reality is that this thing called the Church isn't perfect, and it's filled with people who range from saint to sinner and everywhere in between.

But in the mix is Jesus.

The longer I call myself a Christian, the more I realize what a mess God has to work with at times (myself included), and why it is so important that He remain the apple of my eye. The Body of Christ, when it works scripturally, is a powerful force for change and a light that beckons us to know God, but it will never be ideal. It wasn't without fault in Scripture, and it's not without fault today. Even so, when we take our eyes off of one another and open our heart to a sovereign God, true community can take place.

We are able to give grace to imperfect people (thankfully!) and grow together.

But let's acknowledge that it's confusing when the church breaks your heart—or in Amy's case, her spirit.

So, what does Jesus' example teach us? Distorted religion can hurt your heart, but Jesus reclaims it.

TURN YOUR HEART TOWARD TRUTH

"Turn my **heart** toward your statutes and not toward selfish gain" (Ps. 119: 36). *leb* [Hebrew]; inner man, mind, will, heart—my attention.

In the wilderness, the enemy desperately tried to distract Jesus from His mission. He tempted Him with power. With food when His stomach was clenched tight with hunger. With illusions of glory. Satan reached into the core of every felt need that Jesus was experiencing and dangled temptation with a calculated goal.

Jesus didn't deny that He was so famished that a loaf of bread would be a feast, or that there were times when He would have liked to check out of His suffering (and that to come) and allow angels to whisk Him away. Instead, in that oh-so-hard battle, He simply pointed to Scripture—to truth that even the enemy couldn't refute.

Truth is our first and greatest weapon against spiritual abuse.

Not too long ago, a friend shared that she was struggling with some things that were going on in the leadership of her church. As she talked it through, it wasn't difficult to see that the rules and requirements and teaching were not just restrictive, but manipulative. In this particular church, faith became about pleasing or placating those in power, and Scripture was used to wreak havoc in families.

My friend had often mentioned her "prodigal son." I thought they were estranged as a result of her son's destructive choices, or simply because he preferred to keep his distance from the rest of the family. But she confessed that he had been cut off because he questioned the leader of this church, who declared this young man's questions as sin. The family was asked to keep him at a distance until he showed remorse and came back "into the fold."

The truth had been bent and twisted. Scriptures were taken out of context, and it all held my friend captive.

Ruth Graham, in her book *In Every Pew Sits a Broken Heart*, reminds us: "The premise for entering the church—for deciding to follow Christ—is admitting that we are sinners in need of a Redeemer, that we cannot make it on our own, that we cannot restore our own ruins."[4]

Nowhere in Scripture is the premise for entering a church to lift up a man, or a woman, or to create a closed-in community with special requirements to fit in.

So, what is our truth?

When you follow Christ, there should be no walls that hold you in, isolating you from others who love Jesus.

> Just as a body, though one, has many parts, but all its many parts form one body, so it is with Christ. For we were all baptized by one Spirit so as to form one body—whether Jews or Gentiles, slave or free—and we were all given the one Spirit to drink. Even so the body is not made up of one part but of many (1 Cor. 12:12-14).

Our relationship with Jesus is a personal decision, but it's also a decision to join in with the millions across time—and across nations, races and creeds—who have professed that they believe in Him.

Thank God for beautiful and humble buildings where we congregate to learn and worship together. Thank God that people who want to worship in similar ways can find that congregation. But the true Church of God is so much more vast than this.

Abuse can go in two directions.

> Christ is the head of the church which is His body. He is the beginning of all things. He is the first to be raised from the dead. He is to have first place in everything. God the Father was pleased to have everything made perfect by Christ, His Son. Everything in heaven and on earth can come to God because of Christ's death on the cross. Christ's blood has made peace (Col. 1:18-20, *NLV*).

A pastor or teacher's role is to lead people to Jesus. It's to join in with Jesus' mission and to bring change and life and truth to a community of believers. It's to shepherd.

Christ is the head of the church, and that is where we find our truth, but we also realize that pastoring is one of the hardest jobs there is, and many times a pastor or pastor's family endures spiritual abuse at the hands of leaders in his church, or by members who are demanding or want to have influence in every detail of a church's running.

In our call to honor Christ as head of the church, in no way is this an invitation to place a heavier burden on a pastor whose heart is to love those within his care. We are never to turn our own hearts to spiritually abuse anyone, but we should take special care not to spiritually bully those who have followed God's call to ministry—or their family members. It's simply to give us all a framework of truth on which to build.

Our authority is Scripture (see 2 Tim. 3:16-17).
If a pastor or other religious leader demands that you worship or obey him or her, or if the doctrine they present is confusing and out of context, you have the right (and responsibility) to go back to Christ's teaching. If what your leaders are telling you doesn't line up with Scripture, you are free to leave and find a healthy body of believers with whom to worship.

No person (no matter who they are) should hold the power to keep you against your will in a denomination or church community, or to demand that you adhere to a certain set of beliefs that defy Scripture or that are a limited, out-of-context theology. They shouldn't hold the power to make you feel "less than," or to badger you into doing what they believe is right, or to pressure you to such an extent that you crumble under the weight of their expectations.

We gain confidence in this truth as we study Scripture for ourselves, seek godly counsel (not just from those in authority, but from those who reflect Jesus' teaching), and pray for wisdom. This is not a call to engage in a battle to see who is right. This is about seeking the truth for the sake of our own healing.

My friend studied Scriptures that had been quoted to her in regard to her son, and she found them to be distorted. As she read the story of the prodigal son, she prayed that the Holy Spirit would bring this story to life. For the first time, she wasn't counting on others to spiritually feed her or to be her source of scriptural truth and understanding. Instead, she began to talk with her Savior daily and get to know Him for herself. In a short amount of time, she discovered that the teaching that had been held over her head, and the heads of her family members, was unbiblical.

Like my friend, you are free to search out Scriptures and find a healthy body of believers with whom to worship and fellowship. If you fear the rejection of those who might not like what you are doing, then reassess the power they hold over your heart.

THIS HELPS YOU TO REDEFINE CHURCH

As we search the Scriptures for the truth about what it means to be God's people, we are free to redefine the word "church" to its original meaning, which is "belonging to the Lord."

I am privileged to minister in amazing churches across the nation. I see so much good in these congregations as people assemble to teach and disciple and love one another; as they reach out to others in tangible ways, such as feeding the hungry, opening their homes to those who have no place to lay their head, and raising funds to adopt children with severe needs; and as they simply encourage one another with just the right words.

Every day I slip into a small coffee shop to work. This coffee shop is founded by a church and open to the community, and the conversations of people hungry to know Christ buzz around me as I work. I love it!

I rejoice in the Body of Christ as I see those who work self-lessly—who tirelessly labor in ministry, only to be challenged by difficult or work-in-progress Christians—yet still love what they do.

The Church is a vast, living organism comprised of flawed human beings. People are drawn into the Church in a number of ways, but at the core is the unction to be part of a mission to disciple the nations and to love one another. As a member of that Body, I have a choice as I work alongside others who "belong to the Lord." I can allow broken or work-in-progress or messy people to lead me away from the power and spirit of my faith, or I can see my own work-in-progress heart in the process. We simply will not find a church without varied personalities, or where there are never things that need to be worked out and prayed through.

The Church is a family. Every family I know, including my own, has to work through the good and the bad together if they want to create a thriving environment.

Separating those who were spiritually abusive from the good of the Church helped Amy find her way back home again. She says, "We need to learn to keep our eyes firmly fixed on Jesus, who is the author and finisher of our faith. A person or doctrine is peripheral to our focus on our Savior. That's how a person can avoid having their faith shipwrecked."

Amy was able to redefine her relationship with the Church to being known and loved by God—to belonging to Him.

Sure, we will have the privilege of working side by side with Type A (or if you are Type A, Type B) people, with procrastina-tors, with visionaries, with the bossy or timid or warm or kind people who share our path as we follow Jesus—just as they have the privilege of working alongside us, with all of our quirks and personality traits.

We also have the freedom not to be entangled with or in bondage to those who have exchanged faith for false or harmful doctrine.

Years after that moment in the counselor's office, Amy found a place of spiritual health, founded on truth and wrapped in mercy. She forgave her dad. She says:

> As I prayed for grace and mercy toward him, the Holy Spirit began to reveal a truth to me. One that has helped me in so many relationships going forward. Hurting people hurt people. My dad wasn't evil. I don't believe it was his intention to hurt me. In fact, I believe the opposite is true. He was probably operating on what he had been taught. He was likely very concerned for my soul and trying to protect it the only way he knew how. The Church is full of people like my dad—the walking wounded. Just because someone is a follower of Christ doesn't mean they are not deeply broken.

In Christ, we have hope for healing from spiritual abuse. Amy has discovered that it's an active process that requires the hard work of dealing with the wounds received. It's been almost two years since Amy's father passed away. In the end, he held tight to his wounds and they consumed him.

Amy has compassion for her dad, and she believes that while a church should be a safe and loving environment, at the core it is simply a gathering of people who need Jesus. She's careful not to hurt others, or to carry around resentment toward people who bear Christ's name and don't represent Him well, as these actions just perpetuate the pain. She keeps in mind that none of us has control over other people's choices.

"We just have control over our own," Amy says. "I try to remember that it was the religious people of Jesus' day who beat and crucified Him. May God grant us the grace to say about our religious abusers what Jesus said of His: 'Father, forgive them, for they know not what they do.'"

Today Amy leads a house church in Colorado. She loves nothing more than coming alongside those who feel brokenhearted following difficult experiences with the Church. She delights in leading them back to the heart of Jesus' mission, pointing out that Jesus identified with the brokenhearted. She reminds all of us that in a Church made up of messy people, there is hope as we serve and love one another with humility, standing upon a solid Rock that will never give way beneath our feet.

JUST *You* AND *God*

1. In Matthew 23:1-4, we read about religious leaders who laid heavy burdens on people by asking them to do what they themselves were not willing to do. What other warning signs does Jesus describe in this passage?

   _____

   _____

   _____

2. Contrast the burden described by Jesus in Matthew 23:1-4 with the one described in Matthew 11:30.

   _____

   _____

   _____

3. Jesus willingly walked into the wilderness because He was led by the Holy Spirit (see Matt. 4:1-11). As you read this story, what characteristics do you find in Jesus?

_____

_____

_____

_____

4. If you have been hurt in the name of faith, let's get to the heart of the hurt, rather than focus on the individual(s) who caused your pain. Read the following Scriptures. Which of these apply to you? Let it/them soak into those broken places in your heart. Write a prayer asking for what you need today.

- I feel that following Jesus is too hard—read Matthew 11:28-30.
- I don't know if Jesus loves me—read Romans 5:8 and Romans 8:37-39.
- I want to make them pay for what they've done—read Romans 12:19.
- I'm such a mess. Is there hope for me? Read 2 Corinthians 5:17.
- I want to show Jesus' love, but I don't know what it even looks like—read 1 Corinthians 13:4-8.
- Do I matter in God's plan for the Church? Read 1 Corinthians 12:27.

_____

_____

_____

_____

_____

5. Maybe you've encountered people who weren't Christians who were unfair, or who were heavy-handed in discipline and light in mercy. You don't like it, but it's not devastating. Often, our spiritual pain comes from the fact that we just don't expect God's people to behave as if they are without Christ in their lives. How does viewing believers who have hurt you as broken, a work-in-progress, or "messy" affect your view of what happened? How does it affect your view of the Church?

_____

_____

_____

_____

6. If a parent(s) presented an unbalanced (heavy on religion, void of grace) view of faith, or punished you in the name of religion, this can place your focus on earning, achieving and doing rather than on inner transformation. How does shifting your view from the former to the latter change the way you live out your faith?

_____

_____

_____

_____

7. In Amy's case, forgiving those who had hurt her was key in renewing a healthy view of faith. What might it look like to forgive those who spiritually abused you?

_____

_____

_____

_____

THE MENDED HEART PRINCIPLE #3:
TURN YOUR HEART TOWARD TRUTH

We worship *among* imperfect people, but we worship *only* our perfect Savior.

PRAYER

Lord, I was hurt in Your name, and I know that grieves You. If I have allowed that hurt to separate me from Your truth, turn my heart toward Your teachings and grace and truth. You will show me the way and I will run in it!

MENDED HEART CHALLENGE

- If a doctrine or teaching is confusing, dig deeper.
- If an individual demands worship or absolute obedience, redefine their role in your faith and life.
- Forgive those who have hurt you to release the burden you've been carrying.

Notes
1. John Eldredge and Stasi Eldredge, *Captivating* (Nashville, TN: Thomas Nelson, 2005), p. 210.
2. Amy Thedinga. To learn more about Amy's story, visit her website: http://www.amythedinga.com/ (accessed October 2013).
3. Stephen F. Olford with David L. Olford, *Anointed Expository Preaching* (Nashville, TN: Broadman & Holman Publishers, 1998), p. 223.
4. Ruth Graham with Stacy Mattingly, *In Every Pew Sits a Broken Heart* (Grand Rapids, MI: Zondervan, 2008), p. 57.

4

When You Lose a Piece of Your Heart

For a while I sat with Mary and Martha. I'd seen their tears flow at the death of their brother, Lazarus, but what arrested me was seeing their confusion and hurt at how long it took Jesus to get to them. I recognized those feelings.

SHEILA WALSH, *BEAUTIFUL THINGS HAPPEN WHEN A WOMAN TRUSTS GOD*[1]

Colorful balloons and gerbera daisies filled the stage; beautiful floral arrangements and potted plants marched up the steps and covered every space at the front of the sanctuary. There were tears in the audience, but no articles of black clothing in sight. Amber, Callie's mom, had asked that everyone wear something bright and cheerful—something that would have made her feisty, beautiful eight-year-old girl happy. At Callie's funeral, many didn't know what to say, so they offered words that were meant to comfort Amber, but which fell flat on a mama's heart:

- *Callie is in a better place.*
- *I'm so glad that Callie is no longer hurting or suffering.*
- *God must have had another plan for Callie.*

- *Heaven needed another angel.*
- *God will never give you anything more than you can handle.*

As a believer, Amber knew that Callie was in heaven, but that knowledge didn't change the emptiness she felt or the aching that wouldn't go away. People's well-meant words were not soothing, but only made her ache more; often they made her downright angry.

Callie had been fighting for her life from the moment she was born. This angel was courageous, but it was her quick wit and spice that drew people to her. The day she died, doctors took Callie off of life support and placed her in Amber's arms. Surrounded by family and friends, this grieving mother knew that her daughter was already on the way to be with Jesus, and suddenly the only person in the room who mattered was Callie.

The warmth of her was a gift. Every breath was a sound of heaven. Amber took time to memorize her daughter's beautiful face. She ran her fingers through her hair, feeling the texture and promising never to forget. Callie had lost her hair twice in her eight-and-a-half years, but now it was long with a twist of curls, and beautiful in her mother's hands. Amber sang Callie's favorite song, "How Great Is Our God," over and over; kissed Callie on the cheek, forehead and hands; and then sang "Jesus Loves Me." She held her for an hour and a half . . . until Callie took her final breath, even as Amber begged God not to take her.

Once Callie had passed away, Amber held her for another hour, until the funeral home staff came to take her away. Her precious daughter was now with her Creator—her amazing God. But when Callie died, a piece of Amber's heart went with her.

Months passed, and then somehow it was the one-year anniversary of Callie's death. A friend said, "You did it! You conquered all of the firsts without her; it will get easier now."

Just one more comment to which Amber had no words to respond. She knew the statement was well-intentioned. Inside, however, she was screaming, *You still have all of your children. You have no idea how this feels! Every day is just one more day that I do not get to hold my daughter, and it doesn't get easier.*

Not one bit.

WHEN WE LOVE MUCH, WE GRIEVE MUCH

Karla Kay, in *Grief: The Universal Emotion of Loss*, says:

> The ocean is a wonderful metaphor for the experience of grief. It is the expanse of the water, the sound of the surf crashing down and the stillness of the beach. Life is like the surf moving at its own will—endless waves finding their way onto the shore and the mix of sand and stones moving out from underneath our feet. We never know what the waves are going to do, how powerful they will be, if they'll knock us down or lift us up. There are days we cherish and want to remember and there are the days we want to forget forever.[2]

When Amber lost Callie, her little girl was only eight. She suddenly understood how out of order it is for a child to go before a parent. She felt lost, even though she was surrounded by people who loved her. It surprised her how life kept moving—how other people continued to live, breathe, go to work and attend church in the days after Callie's death, while her life halted.

Why, God, why? Why my baby?

Amber thought of all the children who were abused, neglected or unwanted, and she questioned why God hadn't taken them home to ease their pain and saved her little girl instead. She asked

God a hundred times a day what she had done wrong, or why He hadn't taken her in her daughter's place. Grief was a constant companion, and it seemed to have a hundred different faces. Some days, Amber woke up praying that God would take her home to be with Callie. On other days, like her daughter's birthday or holidays, Amber was so emotionally overwhelmed that she wasn't sure how she would make it.

Elizabeth B. Brown, in *Surviving the Loss of a Child*, describes this state of being: "Shock is the initial reaction to a child's death. It is as if you are an observer, allowing you to check out of the emotional chaos temporarily."[3]

Like many bereaved parents, Amber had support during and in the weeks following the event. But then those around her moved back into the regular rhythm of work, church and life. This created a challenging emotional dynamic as others were back to "normal," but Amber felt like normal might never come again. She learned to accept hugs and nod as people talked. She smiled, though the ache was so great that she didn't know how she would draw her next breath. She looked for the good in every day, and she tried to fully love her husband and her small son, even as her heart continued to break.

GRIEF DENIED

Grief pushed down doesn't go away.

Untended grief doesn't have an opportunity to heal, and it may build until it can't be pushed down any more. In Amber's case, it all would come out—the whole range of emotions—in places where she didn't want it to, and in ways that she didn't understand or expect. These kinds of outbursts can leave a grieving person trying to make everyone else feel better—assuring them that he or she is okay.

Many days started well for Amber, but then she would run into a snatch of a song, or a sight that triggered a memory of her little girl. Two years after Callie's death, her bedroom door remained closed. Amber went in from time to time. On easier days she sat on the bed and reminisced. On other days she could hardly stand to peek in. The pillow was a reminder of Callie's curls strewn across it; it was as if Amber could listen and hear the soft sound of her daughter's breathing.

Amber is a friend, and I wept as I read the intimate details of this beautiful mama saying goodbye to sweet Callie. I remember when Callie first came to our church—how she used a walker at such a young age, and how her parents fought to find the right treatment to battle the metabolic gene disorder. I remember when she started getting better, and how many of us in the church clapped the day she walked down the aisle with no walker in sight.

I can picture Callie's smile that disarmed those who first met her, and how she surprised people with a zinger that made them laugh out loud. I can still see her raising her hands to worship God on Sunday mornings, tucked close to her mom's side.

At the funeral I pulled Amber in my arms, but I didn't really know what to say to her. It's hard to find the right words in the face of such great loss, especially when it feels as if a prayer has gone unanswered.

The Jesus Factor

In John 11, we find Martha and Mary mourning the unexpected death of their brother, Lazarus. Earlier in the week, Martha had sent word to Jesus that Lazarus was deathly ill. Jesus was making His way to their home when He turned to His disciples and told them that Lazarus was in a deep sleep. The disciples were encouraged to hear that Lazarus was sleeping, thinking perhaps he was on the mend.

Then Jesus put it in plainer language: "He's dead."

Four days later, Martha, hearing that Jesus and the disciples are approaching the city gates, rushes out to meet Him.

"Lord, if you had been here, my brother would not have died. But I know that even now God will give you whatever you ask" (vv. 21-22).

Martha's reaction to Jesus is a mixture of faith and taking charge, not surprising given what we know about her. What captures my attention more in this story is the reaction of Mary—because she's not there.

Mary . . . who sat at Jesus' feet at a dinner party, vexing her more industrious sister because she wasn't helping in the kitchen.

Mary . . . who eagerly listened to every word that came from Jesus' lips.

Mary . . . who loved Jesus as a sister, but more deeply as her Lord.

"Where's Mary?" Jesus asks.

Martha tells him that Mary remained behind. Jesus asks her to go get her, and Martha rushes to her sister to convey the message. Mary stands up from her vigil of mourning and makes her way to Jesus. In that day, the bereaved family's neighbors and friends would join the family in the act of mourning, literally weeping aloud outside the door. When Mary arises, the mourners believe that she is on the way to her brother's tomb, and they follow her through the city streets, their keening sounds of sorrow announcing her grief to the world at large.

Mary approaches Jesus and falls at His feet.

"Lord, if you had been here, my brother would not have died" (v. 32).

Where were You?

Mary doesn't exactly ask that question, but her message is clear. She presents her grief with open hands and a tear-streaked face.

Looking at Mary—His friend, a disciple, a woman who loves much—"Jesus wept" (v. 35). Scholars describe this simple sentence as evidence of a man deeply troubled and moved. One commentary describes Jesus' weeping as an "expression of the Divine in contrast to the human spirit."[4]

Beyond mere empathy, Jesus was so moved by the depths of Mary's sorrow that God Himself reached from heaven to weep with her. The writer of Hebrews says:

> Therefore, since we have a great high priest who has passed through the heavens, Jesus the Son of God, let us hold fast our confession. For we do not have a high priest who cannot sympathize with our weaknesses, but One who has been tempted in all things as we are, yet without sin. Therefore let us draw near with confidence to the throne of grace, so that we may receive mercy and find grace to help in time of need (Heb. 4:14-16, *NASB*).

Many times this passage is taught in reference to sin, but in context, the author of Hebrews is assuring us that we do not have a Savior who is unsympathetic to our deeper moments of pain. He suffered and celebrated the full range of human emotions. With this understanding, He invites us to step into His presence, where mercy and grace await to help us in our times of need.

When you lose someone you love, a piece of your heart goes missing. Jesus offers inner peace rather than inner anguish as He grieves with you.

> **Pierced. Crushed. Wounds. . . .**
> Words that denote the condition of the Servant
> on our behalf. As a result those who believe in
> Him have inner peace rather than inner anguish
> or grief and are healed spiritually.[5]

HIS GRIEVING WITH YOU MEANS YOU ARE SEEN

When you have suffered a great loss, you can begin to feel invisible.

Sheila Walsh, in *God Loves Broken People*, shares a poem written by Stevie Smith, a British poet. Smith describes a man far from shore, waving for help because he is drowning. People pass by and wave merrily back at the man, not realizing that he is actually in trouble. Sheila could identify with this image; she says, "Sometimes I thrust my hands up in the air, my arms flailing wildly, and people nod and smile and return what they see as a wave. But I'm not waving. I'm drowning."[6]

Grief can feel like that. When Jesus wept, His response was compassion, but it went far deeper than that. He identified with Mary's pain as God. He identifies with your pain the same way. He sees you waving. He knows that you are tired. He weeps with you, but He also stands in place to be your lifeline—to walk into the depths of your grief and carry you back to shore.

> Surely he hath borne our griefs, and carried our sorrows: yet we did esteem him stricken, smitten of God, and afflicted (Isa. 53:4, *KJV*).

Isaiah's prophecy foreshadows Jesus—and His mission, which was fulfilled on the cross, where He felt the weight of heartache as an intimate companion to His suffering. In order that we might be healed, He experienced a sorrow greater than anyone had ever known.

He sees your hurting heart. He sees you. You don't have to wave your arms wildly anymore. He reaches for you; in fact, He walks into those waters to rescue you.

HIS GRIEVING WITH YOU MEANS YOU ARE HEARD

Not too long ago, I stood in the sanctuary of a church in Oklahoma where God's presence was tangible. I had just shared a message on spiritual rest, and many of the 600 women present rushed forward, spiritually tired and hungry for what Jesus was offering.

One woman from that day stands out in my memory. She had lost her son the year before. He was a victim of a senseless and cruel robbery. He and his girlfriend went to a park; in broad daylight, they were robbed of their cell phones and then shot for no apparent reason. As this mom told her story, unvoiced grief lingered around the edges.

She was strong, no doubt. Just the fact that she got up day after day—and held tightly to her faith in spite of this pointless crime—demonstrated strength beyond what most of us possess. As the moments passed, she began to speak out loud her painful thoughts and questions. In the beginning, she hesitated, as if those thoughts were too big and scary to voice out loud.

Just like Mary, she loved Him intimately, but her heart hurt.
Oh, heavenly Father, this is so hard.
I miss him so much. Every day.
How can I find purpose in this?
How can I find You in this?

When I am in the presence of someone who has experienced such terrible loss, and even as I pen these words, my face is upturned to God and my heart is deep in Scripture. My great fear is that I might in some way diminish a person's grief. So I turn to Jesus' example.

What does the Jesus factor show us in the face of loss and grief? That He hears us. You don't have to hide your grief from Him. He soothes your inner anguish, gradually exchanging it for inner peace as He offers a safe place to mourn. Which is not to say there's a 1-2-3 blueprint that ensures you'll be better tomorrow. When you love a person deeply and you lose them, on this side of heaven there will always be a missing piece. That sense of loss remains a part of who you are, because the person you have lost is a part of you.

In His presence, you are not required to hide your grief, or bury it, or pretend it doesn't exist. You don't have to numb it. Escape from it. Rise above it. None of these is required by your heavenly Father. He not only sees you, but He also listens to you.

When I shared this with my friend Amber, she said, "This is so freeing for me. I can cry and not be judged for it."

Sometimes people are not sure what to do with your grief. That your Savior is not afraid of your sorrow, in itself, begins the mending of your heart, for you are invited to express it with the One who was wounded, broken, and carried our sorrows upon Himself on the cross. That sorrow so marred His appearance that He was described as despised and rejected, having no beauty or majesty about Him (see Isa. 53:2b-3). He understands what you are trying to say, even if you can't come up with the words to describe it. You are free to honor the love you have for that loved one as you express it to One who hears you.

It's vital that your grief not be downsized to make another feel comfortable. Nor should it be explained away with pat answers.

This happens; more often than not, it's not an attempt to hurt you, but simply an imperfect human response from those who care. You quickly learn that not every person is a safe place to express your grief or questions. They love you, or care about you, or perhaps just know about you or your loss, but they do not know what to say to you in this season.

But there is a safe place for you.

Does this mean that God will not use people to come alongside you as you mourn—and over time, as you heal? Of course not, but this safe place in Him offers you the opportunity to experience the compassion of God's people in a greater measure.

It also allows you to give grace to those who love you but don't know how to make you feel better, or sometimes even say things that make you feel worse. In Amber's experience, knowing she had that safe place with God gave her the strength to ask people for what she needed when they didn't know what that might be. She says:

> The most helpful thing that helped me grieve was when people just listened. When they weren't judgmental and didn't try to fix me. They didn't give advice when they had never walked in my shoes. They were simply there, and let me cry when I wanted to cry.

Amber began to surround herself with those people, which was important, for grief can often lead to isolation. Her safe place with God also helped her to take words that might inflict pain on an already broken heart, and to give them their proper place in her grief. People loved her but didn't know what to say. Perhaps they were trying to ease the five minutes of pain they felt in the company of her grief. It wasn't her job to teach others how to grieve with her, but it was okay to move toward those who brought her genuine comfort, and to share her needs with those who loved her.

However, the most powerful gift Amber found was in throwing open the door to her grief and inviting Christ in.

HIS GRIEVING WITH YOU EXPANDS YOUR HEART

Jennifer Kennedy Dean, founder of The Praying Life Foundation, is not unfamiliar with unwanted grief. "Life can change in the space it takes for a neurologist to finish a sentence. As short an interlude as is required for breath between words, and the sentence you thought would finish with hope, instead ends with 'no cure, no treatment,'" she says.

Years earlier, Jennifer had felt the Lord leading her to a praying life, rather than just to have a prayer life. As she established this new ministry, her husband, Wayne, was at her side. He was a fellow learner, sounding board, advisor, protector, and her biggest cheerleader. He willingly took on the extra work that fell to him while she made deadlines and traveled to speak, saying that it wasn't a burden because it meant taking care of their three young sons—his favorite thing to do.

Later, Wayne took a huge leap of faith and left his career to be a full-time manager and president of the ministry. No paycheck. No company car. No company-funded trips. Just three little boys and a wife he believed in. Working side by side, and praying through every decision and redirection along the way, Jennifer and Wayne grew the ministry from a corner of their dining room to a full-time ministry with office employees and volunteers.

In October 2005, they sat in a doctor's office, trying to get an answer about the dizziness that had been diagnosed as an inner ear infection but wouldn't go away. The answer they received was the news that Wayne had aggressive brain cancer.

For the next two months, Wayne kept a blog chronicling his illness so that colleagues and friends could stay informed. When an entry was added, usually by Jennifer, it was generally more bad news. Still, Wayne would always say, "But tell them it is well with my soul."

He passed away too soon.

When the fog lifted, Jennifer began to realize that she was, in her words, "a widow, of all things."

She could not imagine continuing in the ministry that had always involved both of them. The thought of taking on a new project or coming up with a fresh idea seemed impossible. She couldn't even say a whole sentence without breaking into sobs. The only time she felt strong was when she was speaking at an event. It was as if a special strength came over her—but then she went back to being a "widow" when she stepped away from the podium.

Jennifer didn't leave her house for minor things, because she never knew what memory might ambush her and send her into a tailspin in public. She explained to her friends and her sons, "A widow lives in my body and I don't know her. I don't know how she'll act. I don't know what to expect from her. I can't let her out in public."

The next Christmas, Jennifer and her grown sons prepared to attend Christmas Eve services—one of Wayne's favorite things. Her sons were not used to having a mom who cried all the time, and they hovered around her, frequently asking, "Are you okay, Mom?"

It hit her.

I'm fragile.

She'd never been fragile before.

In her ministry, she had always taught that embracing the pain of crucifixion was the only path to resurrection. By that she had meant that as we identified with the pain suffered by Jesus, we would discover the life that He offered through that pain.

In the midst of her own sorrow, she wondered if she should have added, "except if your husband dies unexpectedly."

That led to new questions for her.

What if she started embracing the pain, rather than seeing it as a stranger? Would doing so lead to life? Was there something in the midst of her pain that only Christ could give her?

These questions aren't easy ones to ask or answer, but Jennifer started to consider the gifts in the midst of her grief.

She wasn't trying to dismiss the loss of her husband or come up with answers to smooth away the rough edges of her pain. She truly wanted to see if there was something good to be found as she walked this path. She hadn't chosen it; but now that she was on it, she couldn't not follow it. So what did her faith offer her along the way?

Jennifer says, "I realized that the immense loss of Wayne made me desperately dependent on God in ways I had never known otherwise." She found comfort in a Savior who pursued from the cross, knowing in advance that we would all need Him in our hour of unavoidable pain.

Eight years have passed since Wayne's death.

"The widow and I have integrated," Jennifer says. "I'm not fragile anymore, but I am patient with others who are fragile. I think it is easier to tell people that we can avoid suffering and be protected from all pain than it is to tell people that pain is unavoidable and is to be embraced for the work it will do in our lives."

Pride, or a mistaken sense that you need to present a perfect front to those around you, can cause you to think of your wounds and scars as something to hide. Something ugly. Something demeaning. Something that lessens your value. Jennifer says:

But look at Jesus. Look at what Jesus thought of His wounds: "Here, Thomas. Look at My wounds. Touch My scars. These are the proof of My resurrection. I bear the marks of death, but I am alive!" Jesus knew His wounds were beautiful. At the places where I am broken, the power of Christ is authenticated in me for others. Where I have submitted to the crucifixion, the power of the resurrection is put on display. I can say, "Look at my wounds. Touch my scars. I have death wounds, but I am alive." I can wear my wounds without shame. They tell a resurrection story.

When you walk through "the valley of the shadow of death" (Ps. 23:4, *KJV*), you completely understand the rugged terrain—and it may seem as though there is no way out of the valley. But as you go through that dark place, you discover that there is a Shepherd who promises to lead you through.

Stephen Levine, in *Unattended Sorrow*, writes, "We find in our pain the pain we all share. Softening around pain with mercy instead of hardening it with fear, the heart expands as 'my' pain becomes 'the' pain. Odd as it may sound, when we share the insights arising from *our* pain we become more able to honor *the* pain."[7]

Though it may seem like an unusual phrase, "honoring our pain" means that, at the right time, our hearts expand with the insight gained in those darker places.

For Amber, the insight gained is the strength she has found in her relationship with God.

"If I have learned anything in the past two years," she says, "it is that grief has many faces. Sometimes grief is just a whisper in my heart, and there are other times that it stands before me and punches me in the stomach and takes my breath away. It is in these moments that I have learned that I can trust in God. He is the only reason I am where I am today."

When grief floods her heart, Amber pictures her daughter raising her hands to worship, remembering how much her little girl loved her Savior. She envisions that same Savior weeping with her, catching every tear and holding her tight until the day she reunites with her baby girl. "Jesus is my Rock. My Healer. I miss my little girl more and more every day, but I also live with the hope of seeing her again," Amber says.

For Jennifer Dean, her heart expanded to appreciate what it means to be fragile, and to offer compassion from the depths of a heart expanded by sorrow. She identifies with the pain of others who are feeling fragile because of loss. She says that her mourning, and the fact that Jesus grieves with her, *altar'd* her life. This led to a book with that same title, in which she describes what takes place when we offer up every aspect of our lives—including the harder parts, like grief—to God. Jennifer says:

> The noun *altar* is usually understood to be a place of worshipful offering. Something of value is offered up and released on the altar. The offerer relinquishes ownership and yields control to Another—a Power beyond.[8]

No doubt, your life was altered by your loss, and that loss matters to Jesus. It's a dark valley you are walking through, but you don't have to do it alone. Keep your eyes fixed constantly on Him (see Heb. 12:2), as you place what is of great value (your grief) in His hands.

JUST *You* AND *God*

1. Have you pushed down your grief so that others might feel less burdened by your pain? What might you do differently after reading this chapter?

   _____

   _____

   _____

2. In John 11:28, Martha told Mary that Jesus was "asking for her." How is Jesus beckoning you to come to Him in the midst of your brokenness? Write a prayer in response.

   _____

   _____

   _____

3. "Jesus wept" (John 11:35). This response has been described as an "expression of the Divine in contrast to the human spirit." Sometimes people do not know how to respond to grief, but Jesus fully understands the weight of sorrow. What might it mean for Jesus to weep with you?

   _____

   _____

   _____

   _____

4. Write the words from the following verses that describe what you need from God.

   - *He offers rest*: "Come to me, all you who are weary and burdened, and I will give you rest. Take my yoke upon you and learn from me, for I am gentle and humble in heart, and you will find rest for your souls" (Matt. 11:28-29).

- *He renews your strength:* "He gives power to the weak and strength to the powerless. Even youths will become weak and tired, and young men will fall in exhaustion. But those who trust in the LORD will find new strength. They will soar high on wings like eagles. They will run and not grow weary. They will walk and not faint" (Isa. 40:29-31, *NLT*).
- *He keeps you company:* "No, despite all these things, overwhelming victory is ours through Christ, who loved us. And I am convinced that nothing can ever separate us from God's love. Neither death nor life, neither angels nor demons, neither our fears for today nor our worries about tomorrow—not even the powers of hell can separate us from God's love. No power in the sky above or in the earth below—indeed, nothing in all creation will ever be able to separate us from the love of God that is revealed in Christ Jesus our Lord" (Rom. 8:37-39, *NLT*).
- *He offers inner peace in place of inner anguish:* "I am leaving you with a gift—peace of mind and heart. And the peace I give is a gift the world cannot give. So don't be troubled or afraid" (John 14:27, *NLT*).

5. When you experience grief, you can gain new insight through the process. Jennifer Kennedy Dean described this as being altar'd. What insight has come to you through your grief? How can this, with God's help, bring comfort to others at the right time? How does it comfort you?

_____

_____

_____

_____

6. Read Job 2:13. If there is a friend or loved one who doesn't know how to grieve with you, but desires to help, how can you share what you need with that person? Write down three ways a friend or loved one can tangibly help you in this time. Share this list with at least one person.

_____

_____

_____

_____

THE MENDED HEART PRINCIPLE #4:

JESUS WEEPS WITH YOU

When you love much, you grieve much.
You are loved much as you grieve much.

PRAYER

Loving Father, who promises never to leave me or forsake me, who understands the weight I've carried, today I invite You to weep with me. I come to You with open hands, ready to receive renewed life in the heart of my grief.

MENDED HEART CHALLENGE

- Designate a specific time and place to express your grief with Jesus.
- Write your thoughts in a journal.
- Each week, go back and note the times you sensed God with you, or any insights that have come over time.

Notes

1. Sheila Walsh, *Beautiful Things Happen When a Woman Trusts God* (Nashville, TN: Thomas Nelson, 2009). p. xv.
2. Karla Kay Whelchel, *Grief: The Universal Emotion of Loss* (Bloomington, IN: Balboa Press, 2012), pp. 5-6.
3. Elizabeth B. Brown, *Surviving the Loss of a Child* (Grand Rapids, MI: Revell, 2010), p. 162.
4. Johannes P. Louw and Eugene A. Nida, *Greek-English Lexicon of the New Testament Based on Semantic Domains*, vol. 1 (New York: United Bible Societies), p. 322.
5. J. A. Martin, "Isaiah," in John F. Walvoord and Roy B. Zuck, eds., *The Bible Knowledge Commentary, vol. 1* (Wheaton, IL: Victor Books, 1985), Isa. 53:5; p. 1108.
6. Sheila Walsh, *God Loves Broken People* (Nashville, TN: Thomas Nelson, 2012), p. 1.
7. Stephen Levine, *Unattended Sorrow* (Emmaus, PA: Rodale Books, 2005), p. 127.
8. Jennifer Kennedy Dean, *Altar'd*, Kindle version (Birmingham, AL: New Hope Publishers, 2012).

5

When Sin Hurts Your Heart

Fear-based repentance makes us hate ourselves.
Joy-based repentance makes us hate the sin.
TIMOTHY KELLER, *COUNTERFEIT GODS*

An affair was something other women did.

It could never happen to Sarah, not in a million years. She held fast to that belief—until she became the other woman.

When her husband had received news of a promotion a year earlier, the prospect was both exciting and intimidating. The promotion meant a move to another state. Sarah had lived life with the same people, in the same church, with the same neighbors her whole life. That was her comfort zone and she was useful there. She was a Sunday School teacher. She served on the worship team. She ministered to women in her community through a Women's Ministries program. Her life was packed full, and she was secure.

As the date to move approached, Sarah determined that she would see this move and promotion as an adventure and join in the excitement of her children, who were 7 and 10 at the time. But not long after she settled into her new home, the adventure started to feel more like an unwelcome journey. Sarah had always considered herself a strong, independent woman—but as a stay-at-home mom, and with her children in school, she was suddenly eating alone and shopping alone. It was not only different, but also difficult.

The house they had purchased needed a lot of work, so she shouldered the burden of contractors and remodeling, while her husband tried to figure out the ins and outs of his new job. Weeks and months passed, and their relationship slowly disengaged as they went on separate paths while living in the same house.

As the one-year mark lingered just around the corner, Sarah met head-on with the temptation she thought only other women experienced.

He was on staff at a church. Sarah and her husband believed in the mission and vision of this church and had often volunteered there, so they had spent a lot of time with him. The man was a dynamic speaker and Sarah admired him; at times, she admitted later, she almost idolized him. She wrestled with conflicting feelings—caring for him as a friend, but also feeling sorry for him. His wife wasn't involved in ministry because of some health issues, and Sarah often wondered what it would be like to have such a powerful ministry but no one at your side to share in it.

Sarah never revealed her conflicting feelings to her husband. She didn't stop to examine her feelings, or to ask why she was worrying about something as personal as the man's marriage. One day, a crack of opportunity arose—and Sarah walked into a full-blown affair.

Which quickly led to the destruction of the person Sarah thought she was.

SIN WOUNDS

Sin is a topic we tend to shy away from, especially when it's our own. If someone else brings it up, we wonder if they are judging, or trying to fix us or shame us. But what if we could just be honest about it? What if we could be real about the deep roots of pain and regret that sin embeds in our hearts, and about how sin affects us and those we love? What if we could have that conversation, creating a safe place where we say, "I feel this way and I don't know what to do about it"?

Together, we could weigh it and count the cost, and unmask the feelings to look at how sin messes with our lives. We could cast light on the real enemy (see 1 Pet. 5:8), who uses temptation to lure people God loves away from His plan. We could talk about how, when all the pieces fall apart, the enemy pounds a stake into our hearts. We could dig deep together to find the source of our temptation—and then deal with the real issues behind it.

But too often, we don't.

We hide our sin. We play with it in our thought life. We are ashamed to tell others for fear they'll judge us. Or we are so prideful that we pronounce that we are above certain types of temptation (I would never abuse alcohol; I would never have an affair; I would never embezzle money; I would never blatantly lie), even while flirting with the underlying thoughts and feelings that lead from temptation to sin.

When it's all said and done—when the thing we said would never happen, does—we run.

Away from prying eyes and gossip.

Away from admitting our part in the sin.

Away from God.

Away from His healing power.

Once you've made that choice and are fully living out the consequences (whether you've been caught or not), you might believe that there is no way back. That you are forever that woman marked with a scarlet letter.

Are your broken places a result of sin? Perhaps the sin that caused you to feel broken wasn't an affair, but it *was* sin, and you see it clearly now—but it feels too late to do anything about it. Perhaps you've never talked about it. Maybe it's a secret that no one knows.

Not too long ago, I ran into an old friend. We were close way back when. At that time, she was dating a guy no one really understood, because he didn't treat her like she deserved. He also didn't share her faith, which was vibrant—until it started fading, and so did she.

Suddenly she was gone. I heard the rumors that she had an abortion and then moved away, but she didn't respond to any overtures of friendship from those who tried to call her.

When, 30 years later, she walked up and introduced herself at an event where I was speaking, the years fell away. I was excited to see her, but also sad for her. The hurt in her eyes and body language was startling, and it told me that the rumors were true. "No one knows," she whispered quickly. I reached out to embrace her, but she turned away and disappeared into the crowd. She was one of the coordinators of the event, and I tangibly sensed her fear that her past would catch up with her.

I would never have said anything, but just the fact that I knew her story made her stay away from me the entire weekend. My heart ached. Literally, three decades had passed. She was serving God and had a beautiful family, yet that long-ago choice still haunted her.

The secrets of her past were still causing brokenness 30 years later.

What is the dynamic that causes people to feel they have to be (or at least look) perfect to serve God and be accepted in His family? Why is church not a safe place to talk about our struggles and receive grace and support in a loving community? What can and should be done differently?

All of these are important questions, and they should be asked, but the more personal question is:

Why do we carry a burden Jesus willingly took upon Himself?

The cross was costly, and Jesus paid the price in full. The cost of the cross perfectly sums up the price of sin, and the fact that this price has already been paid is very good news for all of us—for Sarah, for me, for my friend and for you.

THE JESUS FACTOR

I love my small group at church. We meet weekly to pray, to grow together in our beliefs, and, of course, to eat! But the first small group established was that of Jesus and His disciples. He poured into this group of men, pulling them into huddles on the sides of mountains, along roads, after meetings, and in the wee hours of the morning. They were free to ask the hard questions, and Jesus answered through parables, direct teaching and example. One day, as the sun rose hot in the sky and the men listened intently, Jesus said:

> You have heard that it was said, "You shall not commit adultery." But I tell you that anyone who looks at a woman lustfully has already committed adultery with her in his heart. If your right eye causes you to stumble, gouge it out and throw it away. It is better for you to lose one part of your body than for your whole body to be thrown into hell. And if your right hand causes you to stumble, cut it off and throw it away. It is better for you to lose one part of your body than for your whole body to go into hell (Matt. 5:27-30).

Harsh, right? This is one of those Scriptures we'd like to skip over; it's most likely not highlighted in fluorescent yellow in our Bibles. The disciples likely received this teaching with the same attitude. As far as we know, these men were not sleeping with women who were not their wives. They had dedicated themselves to following Jesus. They left professions and family and everything that was familiar. And yet Jesus was talking to them about adultery.

GUARD YOUR HEART

"Above all else, guard your heart, for **everything** you do flows from it" (Prov. 4:23). *totsa'ah* [Hebrew]; **everything**: *extremity, outgoing, source, farthest borders.*

Willard F. Harley Jr., Ph.D., founder of Marriage Builders, says that most affairs begin when there is dissatisfaction within a marriage that stems from the failure to meet an important emotional need.[1]

Jesus knew His disciples. He was looking at them as individuals and men, rather than as a group of rule followers. He understood that Peter was impulsive at heart, that James and John struggled with ego, that Andrew lived in the shadow of his more outgoing brother, and that Matthew longed to be seen as a true man of God after betraying his own people as a tax collector for the king.

Temptation has little allure in areas in which we are fulfilled, but it can be awfully seductive in the emotional gaps that we *all* have. These gaps are not limited to marriage.

Proverbs 4:23 says, "Above all else, guard your heart, for everything you do flows from it."

By drawing the disciples' attention to the heart issue, Jesus revealed a deeply personal approach to the topic of sin. In a sense, this conversation created a secure place for His disciples. It also creates a place of security for us. Jesus doesn't hedge around the topic. He doesn't ask us to pretend that because there are rules in place, we are never tempted. He invites us to address the heart issues that may lead to sin—and to guard our hearts against going down those destructive paths.

If you've sinned, and that sin has left you feeling broken, thrown away or rejected, your Savior wants to talk about sin with you. Believe it or not, that's welcome news. He raises the issue not to point out the rules you broke, because you are already perfectly aware of that, but because He desires that your life be transformed.

Jesus knew the weaknesses of the disciples, but He also knew that Peter would one day be respected as a strong leader in the Early Church. That James would be the first to be martyred in His name. That John would pen five books in the Bible. That Andrew would become a fisher of men in one of the larger established churches in Byzantium, and that Matthew would tirelessly preach the gospel in Judea and other countries.

He knows you in the same way. When you have sinned, and feel broken due to that choice(s), it can be easy to feel isolated. You may think that you are the only one who has sinned and that you have lost your usefulness to your Savior, the Church, and those around you.

May I share something? Right now, all around you are women who have fallen short. One of them has her fingertips placed on the keyboard, writing the words you are reading right now. My heart is to serve and love God. But there have been times when I have followed all the rules—and people have called me good—but I have privately wrestled with pride or a critical spirit.

We all have fallen into that crack of opportunity called temptation, which then gave birth to sin and it's lingering effects. This is why we need God's mercy.

Max Lucado, in his book *Grace*, says, "God's grace has a drenching about it.... Grace comes after you. It rewires you.... Grace is the voice that calls us to change and then gives us the power to pull it off." This is a gift for all of us. Grace covers our *big* sins—and our hidden sins.[2]

Suzie, are you excusing Sarah's sin? Are you excusing mine?

No, I'm not big enough to do that, and it's not my job. Together, we're just placing sin out in the open and robbing it of its power. No one is immune from sin. That means we don't have to hide anymore. We can come into the Light with an honest heart and a sincere desire for truth, and we will find renewal, no matter what our sin may be. John 3:20-21 says:

Everyone who does evil hates the light, and will not come into the light for fear that their deeds will be exposed. But whoever lives by the truth comes into the light, so that it may be seen plainly that what they have done has been done in the sight of God.

In that conversation on the side of the mountain, Jesus wasn't asking the disciples to literally cut off their hands or gouge out their eyes. Rather, He was challenging them to be willing to go to the root, because "each person is tempted when they are dragged away by their own evil desire and enticed. Then, after desire has conceived, it gives birth to sin; and sin, when it is full-grown, gives birth to death" (Jas. 1:14-15).

When we realize that our Savior isn't afraid to talk about our sin, we don't have to remain broken anymore. We can embrace the truth that this isn't His plan for any of us. We are free to see sin as a disruption of God's perfect plan, and to stop it at the point of conception, rather than entertain it, nurture it, and give birth to it.

It's not always easy to grasp that His ways are perfect and truly in our best interests, but when we do come to that understanding, it takes the drudgery out of holiness (see Prov. 3:17) and brings life in its place. We realize that God's not on a power trip, saying, "Do this, or else!" He's trying to show us how to partner with Him and have a good life (see Ps. 25:10). When we recognize that He has the absolute best intentions toward us, we become eager to learn His ways and do them, and that brings us straight into the heart of Jesus' mission.

HE SHOWS US MERCY

"But because of his great love for us, God, who is rich in **mercy**, made us alive with Christ even when we were dead in transgressions— it is by grace you have been saved" (Eph. 2:4-5). *eleos* [Greek]; *n*: [**mercy**] kindness or concern for someone in serious need— "to show mercy, to be merciful toward, to have mercy on, mercy."

Most temptation comes at the crux of unmet expectations. We're rumbling along nicely until suddenly our expectations aren't met—in our marriages, as moms, in our jobs, with our parents, in our churches, because we don't feel pretty anymore, or because we are wrestling with that I-don't-fit-in-anywhere feeling that won't go away.

Temptation is a lure because it makes us feel something new, or something that we haven't felt in a long time. It is exciting or tantalizing, so we savor it—just for a moment, and then another. We idolize a mere person, or success, and we move as close to the temptation as we can without actually giving in. We give a person or thing more space in our heart or mind than they should occupy.

When we think of Jesus' mission, mercy is an obvious gift. But what if that mercy comes in the form of opening our eyes? We are blind in many areas, but few so great as the area of unmet expectations.

My marriage is a happy one, so my temptation might be to say, as Sarah once did, "That could never happen to me." But just this past year, two sets of close friends, both married for over 30 years, were devastated by adultery. It was a wake-up call. Sitting in front of my computer, watching as a status went from "married" to "complicated," shocked me.

Richard and I knelt together in prayer, asking God that we wouldn't be unaware that our marriage and our lives are not above temptation. Deep down, yes, I believe that my marriage is strong—that I'm so in love with this guy that it can't happen—but in guarding my heart, I'm not going to pretend that there aren't gaps, because there are:

- I can be hurt when he's silent after a bad week at work.
- He can get so task-oriented that he doesn't take time to play.
- I have a temper that simmers for a very long time, but then can erupt.

It's in these gaps that temptation would like to tiptoe in. Richard and I talked all evening after our friends' marriages fell apart. We discussed those places where we are very human, and how they affect us and our relationship. We thought about ways we could intentionally work through them in a healthy manner, and we promised not to take each other or the strength of our relationship for granted.

I don't share this story to point out that my marriage is better than anyone else's, but rather to say that it's an act of mercy on God's part to shake us out of our "it's never gonna happen to me" mentality so that we might deliberately guard our hearts.

Guarding your heart is no different from buckling a beautiful child into an infant seat, or placing a seatbelt across your own chest before pulling out of your driveway. You aren't going to stay home, wrapped in a plastic bubble, because there's danger out there. But you aren't going to be careless, either. You are going to look for ways to protect what is valuable, understanding that in order to navigate safely, you must wisely use precaution.

You See Temptation for What It Is

Dealing with the issue of sin requires opening our eyes to the fact that there is an enemy who wants to trip us up. The apostle Peter reminds us, "Keep a cool head. Stay alert. The Devil is poised to pounce, and would like nothing better than to catch you napping. Keep your guard up" (1 Pet. 5:8-9, *THE MESSAGE*).

Scripture also tells us that this enemy is a liar (see John 8:44). One way to guard against temptation is to uncover his lies:

- The enemy wants you to isolate yourself when you are tempted or when you sin, but Jesus asks that you bring sin into the Light.

- The enemy desires that you feed the thoughts of worthlessness or "I've already sinned, so why not just stay there?"—but he's a liar, and not the voice to listen to when grace is reaching for you.
- The enemy wants you to keep your hands full of yesterday's junk, but Jesus asks that you live with open hands to receive what He has for you today.
- The enemy tries to convince you that you are powerless, but there is immense power in a mended heart.

Whenever we exchange the truth for a misleading lie, it takes us down a rabbit trail. But when we uncover the lies, it changes the way we address temptation.

Knowing the truth empowers us to view temptation like a fierce warrior. When temptation hits (and it will), we see Satan sneaking up the hill. We understand that he is aware of our shortcomings, and that he fully intends to take us down—to attack our marriage, to slice away our sense of self, or otherwise to lure us toward destruction (see Jas. 1:14-15). But with our new eyes, we remind ourselves of the mercy God extends to us: "But because of his great love for us, God, who is rich in mercy, made us alive with Christ even when we were dead in transgressions—it is by grace you have been saved" (Eph. 2:4-5).

Satan doesn't get to win. He does not get to lead us down a path far from God's best for us, or those we love.

Rather than flirting with sin, grab it by the root. Don't justify it. Don't try to disguise it. Call it what it is—lust or greed or loneliness or insecurity. When you feel tempted to give in to something that you ache for, you can honestly tell your heavenly Father that your desire is to love, serve and know Him. You can ask God to shine a light on the temptation and help you count the cost (see Luke 14:28). You can praise Him for being a safe place where you can be real about how you feel, and you are not turned away or made to feel ashamed about the enemy's lie, but rather you are equipped to resist it.

If your brokenness is due to sin, face it with genuine sorrow and offer amends to those you have hurt, but also accept the forgiveness offered. Ask God to begin to illuminate the source of your emotional gaps, and then open those raw and wounded areas to His touch, no longer making excuses or hiding away because of shame.

Your natural response may be to run away from God, like Adam and Eve did in the Garden, rather than to run toward Him. Refuse this impulse, for it lacks a true understanding of God's perfect love.

There is no fear in love.

And God loves you.

No Longer Trapped

Sarah felt trapped in her choices. She knew that her husband, Jeff, suspected that something was wrong. He later said he didn't know if it was the move or their marriage. Thoughts had come that Sarah might be having an affair, but he pushed that impossible idea away.

They were on vacation, and their children were playing in a wave pool in a water park. Sarah and Jeff sat at a nearby table, watching them.

"Are you leaving me?" Jeff blurted out.

Sarah whispered, "Yes."

"Are you having an affair?"

"Yes." She took one last glance at her children and left without saying goodbye. She grabbed a taxi, traveled to the airport, and flew home. At that time, her plan was to see the man the next morning, with every intention of leaving her husband and two precious children. On the ride home, she felt utterly and completely messed up.

That night, she heard a knock at the door. Jeff had driven all day, meeting his parents so they could take the children to a nearby hotel while he talked with Sarah. His original motive had been to confront the man he held responsible for destroying his family, but the closer he got to home, the more he sensed God asking him to instead confront what was truly destroying his marriage.

Sarah silently listened as Jeff rose the next morning and dressed as if to go to work. She suspected that he was on the way to an attorney's office or to meet the man in person. She had already decided not to see the man anymore, but fear rose, telling her it was too late.

She had lost everything.

Meanwhile, her husband sat outside in the car, his eyes closed, exhausted from the drive. Exhausted from everything that had taken place in the last 48 hours. He continued to feel God speaking to him, telling him not to do what he was getting ready to do. To battle this another way.

Go back inside.

When he did, Sarah was waiting and walked into his arms.

Beautiful, right? It's the happy ending we hoped for when we started this story, but it is also where the harder parts of Sarah and Jeff's story begin. Like an F5 tornado, the affair left carnage in its wake and severely damaged the foundation of their marriage.

For weeks, Sarah was a mess of emotions. Sometimes she blamed the man, wondering how a godly person with such a high position in a church could have crossed those lines. Other times, she pointed the finger at herself, wondering how she had lost her way. She pondered the reasons she had believed him, and then, just as quickly, wondered why she hadn't been strong enough to resist the overtures.

Was she a victim? Was she at fault? How did this happen?

While these may seem like important questions, let's remember how Jesus deals with sin. He peels away the superficial to find the source of infection. Like a skilled heart surgeon, He cracks open the chest to find out which artery is leaking, or which primary muscle needs to be revived.

If you've sinned, you could play the blame game for years—but that won't get you any closer to healing. The key to change is letting God see you completely, no holds barred, and offering up your thoughts, your relationships, your life and your heart to His skilled touch.

For Sarah, walking into her husband's arms was her first surrender. Letting God see *her* completely was the second, and the most painful.

One of God's names is *El Roi*, which literally means "the God who sees." Perhaps this doesn't feel like good news to you. When you've sinned, the fact that God sees can be disconcerting.

Tammy Maltby, in *The God Who Sees You*, says that when Adam and Eve sinned, the couple's first response was to look down in shame at their naked, vulnerable bodies and cover up.

Suddenly there they were, crouching behind the bushes, still yearning to be seen because that need was part of who they were, yet absolutely terrified that the truth of who they were and what they'd done would be revealed.[3]

In an earlier chapter, we discussed how God sees us in the midst of grief, letting us know that we are not invisible. This is a different way of being seen. It's allowing the Holy Spirit to expose the truth of what we've done and show us how we got there. This allows something powerful to take place. *THE MESSAGE* says it like this: "The Spirit, not content to flit around on the surface, dives into the depths of God, and brings out what God planned all along" (1 Cor. 2:10).

When we stop hiding behind our sin, that mistake becomes a teacher. Maltby says that we can hide so long that "we don't have a clue how to reveal ourselves to God or anyone else" and that "staying hidden and secret can be a way of hanging on to control."[4] But what if we exchange hiding for knowledge? God sees beyond the obvious sin to the heart of the issue—and then reveals that truth to us. This leads us to actually address the heart issues beneath, rather than to launch an investigation to place blame or to live in perpetual humiliation.

This is where Jesus led Sarah. With guidance, she began to look beyond the affair to honestly assess the emotional gaps that had made an affair viable to a woman who said she'd never have one. This led to an unexpected discovery: The affair wasn't about a sexual tryst with a guy. Not really, not at the heart of it.

Long before the move—long before she was tempted—a barricade had been erected between Sarah and Jeff. In the early years of their marriage, they went through two traumatic losses. One of Jeff's friends died suddenly, and then one year later he lost another best friend to a heart attack. Each man left behind a wife and kids. Sarah was extremely close to the women who lost their husbands. These losses made her start to believe that she might be next. It seemed silly, but the feelings were real. However, she didn't tell her husband or anyone else how she felt. How do you tell someone that you fear that your husband might die, and that you need to be so independent and strong that you could go on with your two children and be both mother and father?

Because of her fear, Sarah spent the next 10 years teaching herself how not to need Jeff.

She filled that emotional gap with friends, with busyness in the church, with family events and other things. She told herself that she had a good marriage because they didn't fight. But when her comfort zone was stripped away as a result of the move, the walls she had built left her feeling very alone. They also left her husband feeling alone, for the one thing he desired in his marriage was to be needed by his wife.

Until that moment of realization, Sarah would have told anyone that their marriage of 17 years before the affair was a happy one. They didn't fight like other couples. They were great companions. They loved each other and their children.

The unfolding of this revelation was a gift. It allowed Sarah to work on an issue that had nothing to do with her husband, but which affected him and their marriage. In no way was this new insight an excuse for what she had done. It simply revealed a heart condition that needed to be healed.

It also revealed where the foundation for the affair had been laid. The "big" sins in our lives don't happen in a moment. They are the result of hundreds of agreements (believing in a lie contrary to God's best for you) that lead up to the final act. In Sarah's case, the lie was something like: "God's not enough. I won't be okay without my husband, so I must build a structure of independence. God's not my safety net; I must create one for myself."

Let's pause for a moment and invite the Holy Spirit to help us look beyond our sins to the needs beneath. Choose an area of your life where you have fallen short, and ask yourself the following questions:

- What is the obvious temptation?
- What is the underlying issue that needs to be addressed?

- What agreement am I making (believing a lie that is contrary to God's best for me)?
- What is the real heart condition?

There's no way that you can begin and finish this introspection in a few moments, but just reflecting on these questions is a beautiful beginning, for knowledge is healing. It's not a secret anymore. It doesn't have to be hush-hush.

Perhaps this initial self-examination will lead you to a deeper trust walk with Christ as you and He work through the issues He is making known to you. Maybe it will lead you to the office of a licensed Christian counselor who can give you tools to change an ingrained behavior or way of thinking. Perhaps a trusted, godly friend or your spouse comes alongside and provides accountability until you recognize temptation for the lie that it is.

Regardless of how the transformation takes place, you are now addressing what led you into sin, which leads you out. You're not hiding. You are no longer trapped.

YOU CHOOSE JOYFUL VS. SHAME-BASED REPENTANCE

We have the opportunity to choose between what Max Lucado describes as shame-based and joyful types of repentance. In the first scenario, we can hide. We can incriminate ourselves or point the finger at others. We can define ourselves by the sin. We can say we are sorry, and wish it had never happened, but believe that there are no second chances, no discovery process to learn how we can grow through it, and no safe place even in our own hearts for God to touch the brokenness. All of this is fear- or shame-based repentance, and it only leads us to hate ourselves as well as the sin.

The Christian faith offers a second alternative. It's very personal. You acknowledge your sin and open your heart, including the messed-up stuff, to Christ. You accept the fact that He can help you to see what and who you can be.

Good news. Good news! *Good news!*

You run toward Him, rather than away from Him. You know it's going to be uncomfortable learning about yourself, but you believe that it will also be freeing. You know that the process might include accepting consequences, or rebuilding trust, or believing in yourself when others have given up on you—but with you and Jesus, everything is possible.

In this process, restoration begins. The other thing that begins is a series of choices. For Sarah, this meant completely cutting off the relationship with the other man. When we see clearly enough to recognize those things that can destroy us or distract us from God's best, there is a definitive pulling away on our part.

It's an act of wisdom to acknowledge that while there's renewal taking place in the ways you think and act, until that healing is complete, your feelings might try to lead you in the opposite direction from what your heart truly wants. Just as we would not dangle our most precious dreams over a yawning pit, so also should we not keep the object of our temptation nurtured and nearby.

Another choice we can make is to strip the secrets of their power. Sarah told those closest to her about the affair. By doing so, she took away its clout to control. She didn't have to hide it for years only to have it come out unexpectedly. She didn't have to live in closeted shame.

This step isn't easy. It was hard for Sarah to sit with those she loved—her parents, a sibling, her closest friends—and share what had taken place. Some immediately tried to fix her. Some were shocked and hurt. A few treated her as if she had made a childish mistake and could no longer be trusted. In this period, she had faith that her honesty with those closest to her was the best decision. She realized that she had held her secret close for a long time, and they were reacting to news that was fresh and unsettling.

One day she sensed God asking, *How can I bless this, My daughter?*

The question came when she was most vulnerable. In the past, her husband would have been so hurt that he probably would have poured himself into busyness, divorced her, or made her leave. Instead, he had chosen to protect her from those who doubted her character, or who questioned their decision to heal their marriage. He had chosen to stay and love her, even though it meant working through really hard issues.

These were beautiful acts, but sometimes they only made Sarah more aware that she had betrayed both her faith and her husband. There were days when she struggled to pick up the Bible. How could she read God's Word when she had broken Jeff's heart and damaged relationships with so many? Some days the shame was too heavy, and though she had heard every Scripture on forgiveness, she felt as if none of them were for her. She couldn't fathom ever being whole again—able to be just Sarah, rather than having her identity tied up in her sin.

God's question persisted: *How can I bless this, My daughter?*

Six months after learning of her affair, Sarah's husband was offered a job promotion that would take them back home again. Once this would have been a blessing—an answered prayer—but it was where people knew her best. It was the place where people would question how she could have had such a private affair with such a public man.

After praying about it, they chose to move back home. In the beginning, going to public places was torture. Sarah often felt that all eyes were on her, regardless of whether there was actually anyone there who knew her. She stopped looking people in the eye, and she didn't linger anywhere; she took care of whatever she needed to do and no more.

Gradually, the answer to God's question began to emerge.

One of the reasons Sarah was able to discern that answer was that she and Jeff didn't try to rush the restoration process. The healing of their marriage took two to three years, and every step was taken with care. God's blessing showed up in the things she learned as she took very personal steps to restore her relationship with her husband, and also to rebuild her faith.

She didn't try to hide or ignore what had taken place, but Jesus showed her ways that she unintentionally did so as she grew through the process.

Have you ever had someone say they were sorry, and yet you knew that those were just words? When we allow restoration to go deep, we journey from remorse to repentance and finally to joy at the freedom of utter and absolute mercy.

Sarah is grateful for the people around her who showed her tough love in those times when she struggled, but she also sensed her heavenly Father with her in every part of those harder moments. She was discovering a relationship with Him that was not based on her sin, but on what He saw in her beyond the sin. He knew who she was and what she was becoming.

As restoration took place, so did gratitude.

Sarah takes nothing for granted. Not her marriage, not her children, and not the new ministry that was birthed out of the restoration process. She never thought she'd be able to do ministry work again, but eventually she and Jeff began to come alongside other couples who were struggling in their marriages.

Then one day Sarah felt called to co-found a ministry that brings awareness to human trafficking. She now travels around the nation to talk to teens about the emotional gaps that can lead us to accept attention that is dangerous. She teaches those young people how to recognize the enemy's lies so that they can hold tight to the truth about who they are to Christ. She does everything she can to help them be safe.

Many years have passed since the affair. Sarah has spent the last several years telling her husband that she needs him.

And she does.

But she needs Jesus more, and recognizing that allows her to address any walls that might try to come up. She doesn't pretend anymore that she's above temptation or sin. Life has taught her differently. The other thing her experience has taught her is that she can invite Jesus in with a sledgehammer to knock down those walls, for she's His girl and she intends to live free.

IS THERE PARDON FOR ME?

If your choices have caused you brokenness, there is always hope.

Yes, there will be hard lessons to be learned as God gently restores your heart. Don't rush that process. No quick apologies so you can move on. Let God take you to the source or root of that temptation.

As you learn, don't rush others who are processing things at their own rate. If your sin has hurt others, those individuals may or may not be ready to accept the fact that you are healing. That's okay. Your healing isn't dependent on others. You may have to work over time to regain people's trust. Even if you don't, you've taken a significant step forward.

If temptation still beckons, strip away the mask of that temptation. It's not about a guy or a feeling or the reward you might think is on the other side. Go past the feelings and weigh the cost. Share your secret struggle with someone whose life reflects Christ, and who desires the best for you. If the enemy still tries to sell you a lie, hold out for God's best, rather than the devil's worst. If the enemy tells you to isolate yourself or hide in shame, remind him that you aren't alone in this battle:

> No temptation has overtaken you except what is common to mankind. And God is faithful; he will not let you be tempted beyond what you can bear. But when you are tempted, he will also provide a way out so that you can endure it (1 Cor. 10:13).

There's pardon for you, and a fresh slate. More than that, there's mending going on so that a stronger, wiser woman of faith emerges on the other side.

JUST *You* AND *God*

1. How does this chapter change the way you view Jesus' teaching about sin?

   _____

   _____

   _____

2. Jesus isn't afraid to talk about sin. In what ways does that offer a safe place when you are tempted?

   _____

   _____

   _____

3. Sarah wanted to debate whose fault her sin was, but Jesus took her deeper to discover the underlying issue. For the next few moments, sit silently in the presence of your God,

who knows what you need before you even ask (see Matt. 6:8). Ask Him to begin to show you your need, and invite Him to perform heart surgery with His healing touch.

_____

_____

_____

_____

4. Temptation comes in those areas where we have unmet expectations. With that knowledge, list one practical way you can guard your heart. List one spiritual way you can guard your heart.

_____

_____

_____

_____

5. The biblical definition of hope is "confident expectation." Read Ephesians 1:18-21. How did Paul define hope in his prayer for the church of Ephesus?

_____

_____

_____

_____

6. Make this personal. What hope is found for you in Ephesians 1:18-21?

_____

_____

_____

_____

_____

122   SUZANNE ELLER

THE MENDED HEART PRINCIPLE #5:

JESUS ISN'T AFRAID TO TALK ABOUT SIN

He is your safe place to find forgiveness,
to grow, and to be restored.

PRAYER

(If you have never spoken to God about your sin)
Lord, today I come with open hands. I hold up the junk and I call it what it is. I don't want to hold this secret in my heart anymore. You'll show me when and how to tell those closest to me, but for today I throw open the windows of my heart and let You in.

(If you have)
Jesus, You knelt beside the woman caught in adultery as men stood poised with large rocks in their hands to take her life. You saw something in her that these men could not see. I am sorry for my sin, but I joyfully repent. Show me how to make amends to those I have hurt, as Your Holy Spirit gently teaches me how to become all that You know I can be.

MENDED HEART CHALLENGE

- Count the cost. (What do you stand to lose?)
- Look in the mirror and tell yourself why this choice is contrary to God's best for you.
- Talk about your temptation (or sin) with someone who loves you enough to be honest.

Notes

1. William F. Harley, Jr., Ph.D., *Coping with Infidelity: Part 1 – How Do Affairs Begin?* http://www.marriagebuilders.com/graphic/mbi5059_qa.html (accessed November 2013).
2. Max Lucado, *Grace: More Than We Deserve, Greater Than We Imagine* (Nashville, TN: Thomas Nelson, 2012), pp. 4-8.
3. Tammy Maltby with Anne Christian Buchanan, *The God Who Sees You* (Colorado Springs, CO: David C. Cook, 2012), p. 22.
4. Ibid., p. 20.

6

When a Thief Steals Your Heart

I know not if tomorrow's way
Be steep or rough;
But when His hand is guiding me,
That is enough.

UNKNOWN

Melissa hardly recognizes the little girl she became in one dark moment. She was walking home from the bus stop—a trip that took less than 10 minutes unless she stopped to talk to a friend or neighbor, which she usually did. One of the neighbors was a retired man who sat in his driveway, waving to all the kids walking by. He was always friendly, and on this day he invited the seven-year-old into his garage.

He said he had candy.

Melissa walked into that garage an innocent, trusting girl and walked out scarred. The *friendly* man had sexually violated her. She was too young to understand what was going on and didn't know what to do when it was taking place. In the dark recesses of that garage, he became someone else once the door closed. He did things she never imagined existed, and made her do them in return. She was terrified. When he was done, he said, "Come back tomorrow."

And she did.

Those experiences left little Melissa feeling stained and ruined. She could never tell anyone, because it happened more than once. She felt it was her fault—even her choice. That's what he told her, and that's what she came to believe.

She felt dirty and ashamed, and the little girl who loved to talk to everyone lost her joy.

As Melissa grew from child to adult, the impact of these events left a huge mark on her identity. She didn't understand how God could ever heal those broken places. She spent many years trying to heal herself, or just make herself feel better, but nothing was enough to meet her needs.

So she perfected the art of wearing masks. On the outside she looked great. However, on the inside she felt completely unworthy of any good thing. When she experienced success, she found ways to sabotage herself or quit. She apologized for being good at things and downplayed her God-given strengths.

How could she celebrate a success or put herself out there as good at anything when all she felt was "less than"?

When Something Is Stolen from You

I was mugged at the age of 17. Some tough girls from a north Houston neighborhood saw a lone girl walking through their turf, and they targeted me. I knew something bad was about to happen, but I was one against many. I tried to nonchalantly walk toward safety, but I didn't know anyone in the neighborhood.

I had left my home in Tulsa to spend a couple of months with the biological father I had never known. That day I walked to a small convenience store to get a drink, and my ignorance of the path I chose was paying negative dividends. After several blocks of trailing and tripping me, the girls circled around me. A few minutes later, I sat on the sidewalk, bruised and scared. They took my purse, a ring off my finger, and my money. It was all I had. They also took something that had no monetary value, but which meant a great deal to me. They robbed me of my sense of security.

Which was already a little frazzled at the seams.

The reason I was in Houston that hot, sizzling summer was that I had nowhere else to go. I had graduated high school, and that meant it was time for me to make my own way. I had worked from the age of 14. I babysat. I worked at grocery stories. I juggled two jobs my senior year. I thought I could make it on my own, except on these particular streets I was defenseless and in way over my head.

I wasn't a fighter. If I could have "worked" my way out of that altercation, I might have had a chance, but in a brawl I simply lost. After my attackers left me, I ran from house to house. Moments earlier, they had been occupied by residents peeking out of windows to see what was going on, but now no one answered their doors.

I learned two lessons that day. One: Run faster when you sense imminent danger. Two: If you are caught, no one will help you.

These are the kinds of lessons that are imprinted on the heart of a woman/child when she is overpowered by someone or something bigger than she is. These painful lessons are hard to unlearn, and they often leave their "student" with an inability to trust.

For Melissa, the fact that she was molested by a bigger, older person taught her that she was shameful. That shame drove her to keep her head down.

Don't let anyone notice you.

You can't succeed.

You aren't worth anything.

These are awful lessons to place on the heart of an innocent child, and it's tragic when, many years later, they are still embedded in that child's grown-up heart.

THE JESUS FACTOR

Jesus' popularity is rising. Crowds wait by the shore, outside temples, and in the streets to catch a glimpse of Him.

They have heard of the miracles. His name is discussed privately in high places and whispered behind hands in the community. As Jesus approaches the shore, a crowd welcomes Him with celebration. They have been waiting, and He ascends into the throng of people. Suddenly a man named Jairus, a leader in the local synagogue, falls prostrate at Jesus' feet.

This is one desperate daddy. His only daughter lies at home, dying (see Luke 8:40-42). We know that he is desperate not only by his circumstances, but also by his posture. No Jewish man—much less a man so respected in his community and synagogue—falls at another man's feet. His dignity is thrown out the window in hopes that he might obtain a cure for his little girl.

Jesus requests that Jairus lead him to his home, and the curious crowd follows. They press close like paparazzi, eager to see what happens next. Along the way, Jesus stops. "Who touched me?" He asks (v. 45).

It seems like a ridiculous question. He and His disciples are hemmed in on every side by a mob of people.

There is another distraught person in the crowd that day. She has bled for years, and no doctors can staunch the flow. In her culture, this condition makes her unclean. She is a social and relational pariah in her own community. She has heard the stories of Jesus and presses in to touch the hem of His garment. It's an act of bravery, for she's not allowed to touch others, and also one of exquisite hope.

In the crowd, she figures, her touch will go unnoticed. Her faith must be strong to believe that Jesus could somehow help her, for no one else has been able to do anything. She has seen many doctors and spent all of her money seeking help. She is desperate.

The moment she touches Him, the blood stops flowing.

However, she has been caught in the act. Because of the nature of her disease, she does not want any attention brought to her, but Jesus isn't moving on. Not only that, but her act of touching Jesus has caused Him to become ceremonially unclean.

Yet there He is, standing in the crowd, asking, "Who touched me?"

The woman listens in as those closest to Jesus try to dismiss His question. They point out that He's surrounded by a massive crush of people. She hopes that He'll listen to them—that He'll understand that there's no way a person can walk through a crowd like this and not be touched.

But she also knows the power she felt when she touched the hem of His garment. He must have felt it, too.

THE POWER OF JESUS' TOUCH

Virtue (definition): Effective force or power.

Christ speaks of virtue leaving him in this story, "not in a way of complaint, as if he were hereby either weakened or wronged, but in a way of complacency.

"It was his delight that **virtue** was gone out of him to do any good, and he did not grudge it to the meanest; they were as welcome to it as to the light and heat of the sun. Nor had he the less **virtue** in him for the going out of the **virtue** from him for he is an overflowing fountain."[1] —Matthew Henry

The word "power" in Luke 8:46 means "the potentiality to exert force in performing some function." As hands and shoulders and feet press against Jesus, something beyond the norm takes place. When the hem of His garment is touched, a miracle occurs. While everyone cranes their necks to see what Jesus is talking about, this woman who lives on the fringes of humanity because of a condition she doesn't want and didn't ask for struggles to understand the powerful force that has stopped her disease in its tracks.

She knows that He knows what has taken place, and she falls before Him. In a rush, she tries to explain why she touched the hem of His garment.

His response is beautiful: "Daughter, your faith has healed you. Go in peace" (v. 48).

These words are not dismissive; Jesus is giving her a blessing. He is publicly acknowledging that things are different now. There is favor for a woman who has experienced years of no favor at all. She is free to rest in the depths of peace.

By calling her "daughter," He proclaims that she is socially restored as well as physically healed. She is no longer an outcast.

Jairus has to be watching all of this with mixed emotions. On one hand, a wondrous act has just taken place right in front of him, but on the other hand, his daughter is at home, on the brink of death.

Can you see him taking Jesus by the arm to convince Him that time is of the essence?

But just then a messenger rushes up. "She's dead," he says to Jairus. "There's no need to bother the teacher anymore."

Jesus continues on as if He hasn't heard. As they approach the house, mourners crowd the door. The little girl inside is dead, just as the messenger said. Jesus asks Peter, James, John, and the mom and dad to go into the house, while He pauses just long enough to admonish the mourners: "Stop wailing," He says. "She is not dead but asleep" (v. 52).

The people laugh at Him. They know what dead looks like.

Inside, Jesus takes the girl by the hand and says, "Get up!" She does, and her astounded parents rejoice.

HIS TOUCH BRINGS US FROM DEATH TO LIFE

Two people in need stood before Jesus that day. One begged for his daughter to be healed, while another was totally in awe of the healing she had just received.

Any number of words could have described what took place as the sick woman touched the hem of His garment. It could be called an accident. A brush of the divine and the earthly. A lucky coincidence.

Any number of words could have described what Jesus did when He took Jairus's dead child by her hand. It could have been described as gently clasping her hand, or lifting it to place it in His own, or even holding it close in sorrow.

None of those are accurate descriptions. When Jesus touched these individuals, something was *seized*. It was not a strength of the flesh, for the touch was mild, but sickness and death encountered the force of the Master as each victim was restored.

When you have been robbed, harmed and stolen from by someone bigger than you, Jesus' mission is to take your well-being back from the enemy and return it with His touch.

WHICH BRINGS OLD TO NEW

A child's chair, painted and distressed in bright turquoise, sits on my front porch. The right leg is cracked. Layers of paint peek through the turquoise—shades of white and some other long-ago color. The bottom of the chair has been removed and a planter put in its place. When I saw this chair in a little repurposing shop in Tahlequah, Oklahoma, I marveled at the price.

Only $30.

My husband laughed when I pointed it out, surprised that I wanted so badly to buy it. When you are in full-time ministry, you count your pennies and make sure that you spend them in places that matter. But I loved this repurposed chair/planter. So he carried it to our car and placed it in the trunk.

As we drove home, I imagined where the chair might have come from originally. Perhaps it was put out with the garbage with a "take me" sign on it. Or it might have been salvaged by a dumpster diver. Maybe it sat at a garage sale with a $1 or 50-cent sticker on it. Can you imagine people walking by it? They see only the cracked leg of an ugly child's chair, or the many layers of peeling white paint. "No one can sit on it," they say. "It's worthless. Not even worth a dollar."

But then the craftsman comes along.

He smiles with joy, because everyone else saw only a cracked child's chair, but the craftsman envisions something different—a new purpose for this throwaway chair. He lovingly picks it up and brings it to his shop. He removes the broken seat and places a rough-hewn planter inside. He applies a first coat of paint, and then buffs and distresses the edges. He adds a second coat, this time a lovely turquoise blue, and then gently rubs sandpaper over the edges until the new paint and the former shades of old paint underneath become an intricate pattern of beauty.

Turquoise. White. Yellow. Old, smooth wood. The crack still displayed, but all of it part of an elaborate story.

Then the craftsman proudly puts a new price on the restored item. What had been discarded is now useful. What once was a broken, old, unusable chair is now a charming planter.

What was once sold for 50 cents or a dollar is now worth 30 or 60 times the value it once held.

On the way home, I picked out bright purple and white vincas with a startling red center. Then, I asked my husband to move the planter from left to right, then back again, on the front porch until I found just the right spot. Once it was situated, the vincas spilled over the sides and front. From that day forward, whenever I walk through my front door, that beautiful chair/planter brings me joy.

Many things can make us feel "less than" or throwaway, but few traumas are as damaging as when our innocence is taken. Sexual sin creates a death or sickness of the heart that says we're not worth anything—that we will never be good for anything, that we are not enough, and/or that we are equivalent to the bad things people have done to us. It can build an emotional void that causes its victim to believe: "I'm cracked and broken, and I'll put my heart in the hands of anyone who is willing to give 50 cents."

Your Savior became the master Craftsman the moment He hung on a cross. He gave His life to prove how valuable you are. He declared to the world, "By my wounds, you are healed" (see Isa. 53:5). He became stained and ruined on your behalf. May I be honest with you? Nothing makes me angrier than when someone points out a damaged human being who is precious to God and says, "Oh, she's incurable. She's damaged goods."

But it saddens me more when I hear a similar statement come from the lips of a woman treasured by God who thinks she is somehow beyond His touch. When Jesus stood outside the door of the dead little girl's home and told the crowd to stop mourning, their response was to laugh. They knew *dead* when they saw it. But Jesus saw what they could not. *Dead* is never a finality in Jesus' language. Bringing people back to life is exactly why He came. His mission is to take what has been declared life-less or stolen or discarded and tenderly restore us.

His touch *seizes* the damage inflicted on your sense of self. It sees the sickness of a world where sin exacts a painful price, and reaches for the one who has been impacted by it to bring him or her back to life.

·Long-term effects of sexual abuse are varied and complex. There are no specifics that define a little girl grown up to become a once-abused woman, for every woman and situation is differ-ent. The effects can range from perfectionism to depression to anxiety to anger to over-control. One former victim may struggle to be sexually intimate with her spouse, while another engages in promiscuous behavior. The problem with trying to define someone with words like these is that the very same woman can be creative, loving, successful, kind, and any other number of positive descriptions.

So can we go beyond the labels for just a moment to talk about the Jesus factor? In not one instance in the entire Bible does Jesus pass by a heart hungry for wholeness and say, "Sorry, she's only worth 50 cents. She's too damaged. People or events have taken their toll on her, and there's nothing I can do."

One day Jesus met a tormented man who came running from a cemetery. The man had often been bound in chains—and not just physical chains. He had a habit of cutting himself with sharp stones. We don't know his complete story, but we do know that he was a danger to himself and others. We also know that after an encounter with Jesus, he was described as a man "in his right mind" (Mark 5:15). He longed to follow Jesus into the boat, but Jesus instructed him to go home and show others what the power of God could do. He was a prisoner set free—an example that there is no person beyond Christ's reach (see Mark 5:1-6,18-20).

We could discuss in depth what is taken when a person is touched in the wrong ways (sexual or physical abuse). But you see, we know that. We understand the bonds that are placed on a person's heart because of what was taken from him or her. Those stories matter, and they need to be told, but what is not talked about enough is that healing can take place.

Perhaps that's why Jesus immediately asked the man from the cemetery to run to tell his good news. He tracks across the miles to his village with a message bursting in his heart:

I once was lost, but now I'm found.

I once was chained, but now I'm free.

Jesus touched me, and I know whose I am.

They had seen his chains. They knew that he cut himself with sharp rocks. They knew of his rambling thoughts and wild speech. But now standing in front of them was a man with a sound mind.

As you begin to replace old lessons with new ones, you find out who you are apart from the stain of another's sin. Your story takes a distinctive turn as new truths replace old, inaccurate perceptions.

- You are beautiful, not because of what you have to give, but because of who you are.
- You have value, not because of what I want from you, but because of what has always been inside of you.
- You are restored and have new purpose.
- I recognize the beauty inside of you. My touch is not harmful, but healing.

These new lessons have the power to completely change each of us. Our internal transformation affects the direction we take in life, which in turn impacts those we love, or those who hear our stories.

LOOKING DEEPER

Dr. Dan B. Allender, in *The Wounded Heart*, asks, "What must be done to lift the shroud of shame and contempt?"

He believes the answer to this question involves a strategy that might at first seem to intensify the problem, which is to peer deeply into the wounded heart. Allender asserts, "The first great enemy to lasting change is the propensity to turn our eyes away from the wound and pretend things are fine. The work of restoration cannot begin until a problem is fully faced."[2]

I invite you to take a moment to peer into your own wound:

- What was stolen from you?
- How has that carried over into today?

When you first ask these questions, the experience might be so painful that your inclination is to turn away. But peering into a deeply wounded heart reveals areas in which your heavenly Father wants to abide and share new lessons with you.

Not too long ago, I found myself at a place of spiritual exhaustion. I love what I get to do, but I had been juggling many tasks for a number of months. It seemed that the more that I did, the more I needed to do.

So, I just kept at it.

Late one night, in a room in North Carolina, I curled up in a ball on the bed. Tears slid down my cheeks as I asked God if I had taken on too much, or if I needed to put something down. I'm not a crier or complainer by nature (I generally look at life as an adventure), so this feeling wasn't something I wanted or was accustomed to—which made me feel even more vulnerable. As I wept, these sweet, gentle words came deep inside of me:

You don't have to do this alone.

I knew exactly what those words meant.

Remember the mugging story I shared earlier? The unhealthy lessons I had learned as a young girl were that I needed to run faster, and that if I asked for help there might not be any coming. These lessons were imprinted on my heart, and they had continued to impact me even though I was now a strong woman of faith.

In this uncomfortable, overwhelming moment, God was graciously lifting a layer away to reveal an area that remained broken.

This was my 50-cent area: I felt unworthy of others' time or effort. Early on I had come to believe that asking for help was bothering others—that if something needed to be done, I should and could take care of it myself. I forced myself to just keep running until I could run no more. This area in my heart and thoughts had remained damaged, because long ago my confidence was stolen from me.

I sent out a private email to close friends and family, asking them to pray with me. I was amazed at how many people responded. Within a couple of days, I had formed a behind-the-scenes prayer team. My spirit was buoyed as I read their prayers that first week, and their support continues to uplift me today. But there was more.

It wasn't hard for me to ask for prayer, but to ask someone to come alongside and help? That was tough! A young woman I had known years before when I was ministering to teens had sent me an email several weeks earlier. She followed my ministry and wondered how she might be of assistance to me. I'd love to say that I responded to her offer quickly, just as I did with those who wanted to pray, but I didn't.

I let that email sit. I had lots of great excuses:

I don't want to bother her.

That's too much to ask of someone.

She sent a second email:

I'm still here, Suzie.

That day I asked her to join me on an upcoming ministry trip. It was nearby; it wouldn't require her to drive a long way or deal with the hassles of air travel. It was a baby step toward inviting help. I wish I could accurately describe how much of a difference her presence made. From beginning to end, the event was easier simply because there was another set of hands involved. She assumed responsibility for the smaller details that consumed so much time. She took ownership of them, freeing me to do what I love best: to speak and pray with women, to hear their stories, and to watch God work!

Afterwards, Crystal and I walked back to our hotel. "How in the world have you been doing this alone?" she asked.

I think the more powerful question was: *Why* had I been doing it alone for so long? Crystal has become a valuable part of my ministry team. She and others continue to bless this grown-up girl who once struggled to ask for help.

I discovered a very powerful truth in this process: Many times we resist God—perhaps we even kick and fight against Him—when all He is doing is trying to give us the desires of our heart. We stay on the same old track. We stick to the old ways of doing things. We offer excuses, even valid ones. We hold tight to old lessons, though we're not that same person anymore.

We shy away from God's embrace, because reaching for the touch of a heavenly Father, when the word "touch" has negative connotations, isn't always easy.

There are trust issues. There are times when the lies of a predator try to knock on the door of our thoughts. That's when Philippians 4:19 becomes our anchor: "And my God will meet *all* your needs according to the riches of his glory in Christ Jesus" (emphasis added).

I could have remained in that same rut, spinning my wheels, trying to do it all, and the result would have been more spiritual and emotional exhaustion. My persistence in doing things my way led to a coming to the end of myself. God knew me.

He knows you.

He knows where you are strong, and where the broken pieces lie hidden. Repurposing our weaker or damaged areas isn't always easy. This is where the sanding and buffing comes into the process.

Like the woman with the bleeding disorder, as I reached for the hem of Jesus' garment, He scooped out the old lessons I had learned and put new ones in their place:

It's okay to ask for help.

I can stop when I'm tired and reassess my needs.

When I trust God, I discover brand new things I didn't even know were possible!

Why do we resist this transformative process so strenuously? Those ingrained lessons are comfortable, even if we hate them. We know what to do, and we know what to expect. As the repurposing begins, we don't know how it's all going to work out in the end, and that makes us uneasy.

But He knows.

As you open a heart that has been robbed to His touch, remind yourself daily that it's not about how you feel right now, but what will come of it. Trust that He's the master Craftsman and knows you well.

You Discover That He's Enough

Today Melissa leads an online Bible study that reaches thousands of women across the world through Proverbs 31 Ministries. She's a mom and a wife. And she's whole! She says that as God peeled away the layers one at a time, one question emerged over and over again:

When she felt betrayed, "*God, are You enough?*"

When she needed to forgive what seemed unforgivable, "*God, are You enough?*"

When she struggled in her marriage, "*God, are You enough?*"

When her mom was dying of cancer, "*God, are You enough?*"

When others didn't recognize her value, "*God, are You enough?*"

When she struggled professionally, "*God, are You enough?*"

When someone she loved used words to hurt her, "*God, are You enough?*"

When her past haunted her, "*God, are You enough?*"

When she was let down and disappointed, "*God, are You enough?*"

Verse by verse, she read her Bible. Though her doubts were strong at times, she held the promises of God close, discovering that whenever she asked this question, the answer was always the same:

Yes, He is.

"Nothing here on earth is guaranteed," Melissa says, "except for one thing: Jesus is with us always. When I began to understand who He is, my doubts began to disappear. He is sufficient; He's enough. I stand on this Scripture: Isaiah 46:3-4 says, 'You whom I have upheld since your birth, and have carried since you were born. Even to your old age and gray hairs I am he, I am he who will sustain you. I have made you and I will carry you; I will sustain you and I will rescue you.'"

Throwaways in God's kingdom?

No way! Just treasures in the making.

JUST *You* AND *God*

1. When someone bigger than you overpowers you in any way, it can make you feel helpless. How might that affect the way you trust God?

   _____

   _____

   _____

2. The woman with the issue of blood had a condition that she could not talk about easily. Have you ever felt that there were things you couldn't talk about, or that would set you apart from others if people knew about them?

   _____

   _____

   _____

3. The word "touched" in the cases of the woman with the issue of blood and Jairus's daughter is a forceful one. Though Jesus' touch is gentle, it's also powerful against the broken places in your life. In what places do you need His gentle touch to powerfully take back what was stolen from you?

   _____

   _____

   _____

4. One of my old lessons was that I should "run faster, and don't ask for help." Describe your old lessons and how they impact you or your relationships.

   _____

   _____

   _____

5. What new lessons did you sense the Holy Spirit speaking into your heart as you read this chapter?

_____

_____

_____

6. Read Isaiah 64:8. Jesus never saw a single person He met as a throwaway; He recognized them all as potential treasures. How do you believe the master Craftsman (or Potter) sees you? What might you come to look like as you are shaped by His hands?

_____

_____

_____

_____

THE MENDED HEART PRINCIPLE #6:
HIS TOUCH RESTORES
Your "old" becomes new in the hands of the master Craftsman.

PRAYER

Father, You do not walk past me. You see the riches inside, ready to burst forth at Your touch. I have no idea where that touch will take me, but I eagerly look toward the new discoveries You have for me. Thank You for touching me in a way that is holy and restorative. Thank You for a fresh new beginning!

MENDED HEART CHALLENGE

Read this prayer, titled "Hug the Little Girl within Me," written by Anita Corrine Donihue, and make it your own:

Dear Lord, hug the little girl within me—the little girl mistreated and abused. Encircle me with Your ever-lasting arms. Still my silent sobs. Anoint my head with Your healing oil; free me from nightmares of memories. Touch my scars with Your healing stripes. Soothe each muscle that suffered in anger and pain. I know You suffered, too. Piece together my broken heart. Your heart bled and You died for me. In sleepless nights, wrap me in Your comforting presence. Let me rest in the shadow of You, the Almighty. Hug the little girl in me as You cover me with Your feathers like a mother hen does her chicks. I find refuge under Your wings. Help me to face yesterday (wrong as it was), to forgive as You forgive me, and to look toward tomorrow with hope.[3]

Notes
1. Matthew Henry, *Complete Commentary on the Bible*. http://www.studylight.org/com/mhm/view.cgi?book=lu&chapter=008 (accessed October 2013).
2. Dr. Dan B. Allender, *The Wounded Heart* (Colorado Springs, CO: NavPress, 2008), p. 14.
3. Anita Corrine Donihue, *When I'm on My Knees* (Uhrichsville, OH: Barbour Publishing, Inc., 1997), p. 83.

PART 3

Moving Forward

7

Momentum

Transforming the effects of the fall and growing in the image of God is not an easy task. But God has promised us that the "good work" he began in us, he will carry "on to completion until the day of Christ Jesus" (Phil. 1:6).

HENRY CLOUD, *CHANGES THAT HEAL*[1]

The smooth wood of the altar pressed into my forehead. My tear-streaked face was hidden from those around me, but not from God. I was a young mom in my late twenties, and God was doing something special in my heart. I didn't know how to fully lay claim to it yet; I just knew it existed. Many of the emotional ties to my past had been loosened, and I was changing bit by bit. There were moments when I was surprised by unexpected confidence or a peace that swirled deep inside of me, like a cleansing rush. When I looked in the mirror, I embraced the message that my life was of value to Him. Momentum was taking place in my faith, and in my personal and spiritual maturity.

Momentum is simply the process of moving forward. There's no speed limit, and it's not a race. Momentum is uniquely individual, but it's also a partnership with God; it's a "stake in the ground" conviction that resides inside of you and says, "This girl isn't going to be stuck anymore." The wonderful thing about momentum is that you, and others, may notice progress. The bad thing about momentum is that your progress may be made in such small increments in the beginning that the process causes you angst.

You may want to take things into your own hands and rush the process. Or perhaps you ask God or other people for a specific set of goals so you will know what comes next. You may be waiting quietly on God to show up, but at the same time, you are wondering, *How long?*

This is exactly how I felt that day as I lingered at the altar. All of these emotions and questions rushed through me at once.

What's next, God?

What do You have for me?

Should I be planning, preparing, doing something?

If we aren't careful, we can easily forget the principle in chapter 1: The power of the Cross is not found in what we do, but in what has been done for us.

We can rest in that. God will complete the work He has begun in us. Let's be realistic about the challenges, but also rest in the truth that He's at work. We began by looking at what Jesus has already accomplished for us, and we transitioned to examining a heart in the midst of mending. Now, as we move toward what we can do as we heal, we must keep in mind that we labor in tandem with Christ. We are seeking rather than striving. We are responding in obedience, but the end goal isn't to achieve success in place of failure. The goal is simply to trust.

Momentum leads us to a series of crossroads—places where crucial decisions are often made, but with God's help. Let's begin to consider what momentum looks like in these crossroads, how we might respond in each, and what to do when we aren't sure how to take the next step.

MOMENTUM CAN FEEL AWKWARD

I know awkward well.

One Wednesday night, I was standing in the hallway at church. Across the hall, I saw someone new. I made my way over to her to welcome her, and as we chatted I noticed that there was a long eyelash on her cheek.

There's that old girlfriend rule that if you can't do anything about it, you say nothing, but if there is—like when there's toilet paper stuck to your friend's shoe or broccoli in her teeth—you help a girl out. So I casually reached over as I said, "There's an eyelash on your cheek. Let me get that for you." I went to brush it off and somehow grasped that small hair—and to my absolute dismay, that small eyelash unfurled to about a half-inch long hair . . . attached to the woman's face.

There I was. There she was. Connected by a single hair on her face.

Inside I was screaming, *Let go, let go, let go!*

I'm sure she was thinking the same! *Let go, let go, let go!*

I finally let go, and she took a huge step back as I apologized. She was gracious, even laughing at my *faux pas*. Somehow we ended that awkward conversation and I turned to leave.

I walked down the hall, around the corner, out the double doors and climbed into my car. Church hadn't even started yet, but I was done.

There are those awkward moments that turn out to be ha-ha funny (at least years later), and then there are those that are simply awkward. I've experienced both.

Momentum can be awkward, too, and it's usually not the ha-ha funny kind. You've been moving forward. You tangibly sense what God is doing, but you aren't sure where to go next, or which way to turn when you feel God calling you to bigger and greater things. Do you wait, plunge ahead, or just turn around and make your way back to familiar territory?

There are three crossroads you may encounter in momentum.

WHEN YOU NEED TO MAKE A U-TURN

Saul is on his own mission. He is bustling toward Damascus to arrest followers of Christ. He's a zealous young man who has built a solid reputation among the religious leaders of the day. His name is lifted high in important circles, and it's whispered that this is the guy to watch.

Talk about momentum! He's on the move, but unfortunately he's headed in the wrong direction. Just as the high priests and government authorities know his name, so too do those he has arrested, beaten or jailed. He's greatly feared among those who love Jesus.

On the road to Damascus, a blinding light stops Saul in his tracks. Something, like thunder, is heard in the sky.

"Who are you, lord?" Saul asks (Acts 9:5, *NLT*).

It's interesting that some translations of this verse use a lowercase "l" in the word "lord." Paul's not sure what that sound was in the sky. All he knows is that he's blind, and that something or someone bigger than he is has stopped him cold. "Who are you, lord?" is a question of fear mixed with respect. He doesn't have to wait long to discover the Source.

"The voice replied, 'I am Jesus, the one you are persecuting! Now get up and go into the city, and you will be told what you must do'" (vv. 5-6, *NLT*).

Rather than arriving as the fierce warrior he thought himself to be, Paul is led by the hand into Damascus, where, for three days, he exists in darkness. He doesn't drink or eat. Meanwhile, a godly man named Ananias has a vision and is asked by the Lord to speak to Saul. Ananias's response is dread, and with good reason.

This man, Saul, is backed by the chief high priests. Ananias is no stranger to the reports of those wounded or beaten or dragged from their homes in front of their wives and children as this man stands by and watches.

I can't help but love the obedience of Ananias. In spite of his fears, he makes his way to the now confused and distraught persecutor of the fledgling Church—and he prays for him:

> Then Ananias went to the house and entered it. Placing his hands on Saul, he said, "Brother Saul, the Lord—Jesus, who appeared to you on the road as you were coming here—has sent me so that you may see again and be filled with the Holy Spirit." Immediately, something like scales fell from Saul's eyes, and he could see again. He got up and was baptized, and after taking some food, he regained his strength (vv. 17-19).

Saul now has information that he didn't have three days earlier. It has been confirmed not only that it was Jesus who spoke to him on the road to Damascus, but also that God has a plan for him. He has been handpicked to be a messenger of the good news to the Gentiles.

But there's more: There will also be suffering, just as he has brought suffering to others (see vv. 15-16).

Will Saul stay on the path he's been walking?

Will he continue doing his own thing?

Or will he listen to Jesus?

THE JESUS FACTOR

Saul is at a *personal* crossroads. He has been asked to make a U-turn: He has been running down the wrong path, even though his belief is that it's for the right reason. Jesus stops him with a blazing light of glory and a voice of thunder because He knows something Paul does not. One commentator says:

> The most important event in human history apart from the life, death and resurrection of Jesus of Nazareth is the conversion to Christianity of Saul of Tarsus. If Saul had remained a Jewish rabbi, we would be missing thirteen of twenty-seven books of the New Testament and Christianity's early major expansion to the Gentiles.[2]

As your heart mends, there will be moments when you sense that it's time to make a decision—that you have arrived at a personal crossroads. Like Paul, you might be running with all your might down a road that seems right to you. Yet God sees where it's taking you. You sense that internal nudge that says, "slow down," but not necessarily the reason behind it.

A few years ago, a speaker stood on the stage. As I listened, I sensed God speaking to me. It wasn't a blazing light of glory or a voice of thunder, but I knew that He was trying to get my attention.

The speaker had just challenged the audience to put aside anything that might stand in the way of God's best, and I was painfully aware that I had started to devote large chunks of time to things that held little or no value. Richard had gone back to college and had a busy class schedule. We had moved to a new city to be close to the university, so suddenly I had huge blocks of time on my hands. Where in the evenings I used to walk with Richard, or read, or spend time with a friend, I now played games on my phone or computer, or checked Facebook or Twitter, or watched one mindless TV show after another. There was a little place on the couch with a comfy throw that became a type of sanctuary for me.

You might be saying, "Suzie, that's not a big deal. Why would God say anything to you about that?"

You're right. It wasn't a big deal, and I pause as I share this lest some might think that God is a zap-from-heaven kind of God who blitzes a person with judgment because she plays her tenth game of Candy Crush or leaves a status update on Facebook. It's not that at all. It's that our God is such a personal God that He saw His girl—who loves speaking and writing, who loves people, who loves connecting with others—playing one more mindless game, checking one more status update—and getting stuck in a rut she'd one day come to hate.

U-turns are personal crossroads where the God who knows us best invites us to pursue and embrace things of great worth, rather than those that hold little value. Your personal U-turn might be that temptation to give up on this healing business. It might be old habits that create division in precious relationships. It might be sin that you aren't yet ready to let go of. It might be unforgiveness or resentment. It might be that God is asking you to believe in Him and take a huge step of faith in any area.

We all have the opportunity to respond to God in these personal crossroads.

It can be with a little "l," or we can call Him "Lord."

That night I slipped out of the sanctuary. I didn't care that I was a speaker at that event and people might be watching. In a small, dark prayer room set up for the conference, I lay on the floor in the cool darkness and gave it all up to Him.

When I arrived at home, I realized that this was a bigger battle than I had thought. At first I picked up my smart phone or the remote, or I looked longingly at the comfy place on the couch with the slight indentation of my body in the corner. There were times I caved in.

His light continued to shine on this area of my life.

So, I went outside and walked with a friend, or read, or played music and worshiped. For a couple of months, I consciously denied myself in these areas, until they were in balance with the rest of my life. As time passed, I allowed myself to watch a favorite TV show here or there, and on occasion I played a mean hand of Spades—but they were a stanza in my schedule and not the entire symphony.

It didn't take long to see what God had seen and I did not. In the months that passed after my husband went back to school, I had *slowly* started to isolate. *Slowly* I had found that comfy place where I sunk into the couch cushions while life went on without me. *Slowly* I had started reading my Bible only for ministry. I was still reading it daily, but for a blog post or to prepare a message. Somehow the precious time Jesus and I used to share had become work-related.

I didn't know any of this when the Holy Spirit brought me to a personal crossroads that day at the conference. But my Jesus did. Like Paul, I had the option to keep doing what I was doing. Not only that, I could justify it.

I'm in the Word. I'm not doing anything wrong. This is nothing compared to what others do, so what's the big deal?

Or I could accept the invitation to discover more. When we offer up what is of little value, we clear our heart, our thought life, our future and our present to receive what is of greater worth.

What is your personal crossroads?

Maybe Jesus has been gently nudging you in a new direction for a long time. Perhaps, like with Saul, He's calling you to make an absolute U-turn and there's nothing gentle about it. He's commanding that you move from anger to peace. Or from hurt to healing. The command isn't cruel but curative, as He's taking you away from choices that are unhelpful toward those that are in your best interest.

Have you offered up excuses? Are you holding tightly to the very thing that holds you back?

In that personal crossroads, you have the opportunity to take a U-turn into His best for you. What you walk away from might seem small or even silly to others. They may point out that it's no big deal. Or they might tell you that holding on to anger or pain or unforgiveness makes perfect sense because you've been wronged.

I encountered those kinds of comments from well-meaning people in my early U-turns. Let's face it, change can be uncomfortable for everyone involved. The problem is that if I center in only on what keeps me comfortable, it also keeps me stuck. One of the most powerful aspects of momentum is that at some point you get to look back. Hindsight allows you to see that comfy, familiar place for what it is. It's not comfortable at all—not really. It's a place of non-growth.

Hindsight is a reminder of the gift we are offered in the crossroads.

Not too long ago, I sat with a friend of mine. His faith might be described as up and down. His comfy place is anger. He's angry at his ex. He's upset that she ended their marriage, and now she's doing well. He loves God, but his anger keeps him in a rut. He's one of the most talented people I've ever met, but he's stuck, stuck, stuck. He hates that feeling, but as we sat and chatted, I realized that he wasn't prepared to make a U-turn.

He told me, "I give up, Suzie. If I try, it's just too hard. I have no choice."

Yet he had just made one.

He's waiting for someone else to feel miserable so that he can feel better. Or for them to say that they are sorry. I don't want to discount how my friend feels, or the pain that he's continuing to experience 10 years after an unwanted divorce. I know how hard U-turns are.

But it's also hard to remain trapped spiritually and emotionally, when God is tugging so hard to bring you to a U-turn. His earnest desire is for you to discover what lies ahead, rather than to continue to be mired in the past.

For each of us, that U-turn is about momentum.

In my case, my heavenly Father was inviting me to renew the intimacy and strength that only come through alone times with Him. For Saul, He was offering a new purpose in life. For my friend, He's offering the opportunity not to wake up one day a discouraged, tired old man still waiting for others to change or feel as miserable as he does.

What is He offering you?

In momentum there will always be adjusting, pruning and realignment, for we are transforming from old to new. There are going to be things we are asked to put down or walk away from. In doing so, we will discover a life source that feeds our soul, and from which growth and a vibrant life of faith spring. John 15:1-5 describes it like this:

> I am the true vine, and my Father is the gardener. He cuts off every branch in me that bears no fruit, while every branch that does bear fruit he prunes so that it will be even more fruitful. You are already clean because of the word I have spoken to you. Remain in me, as I also remain in you. No branch can bear fruit by itself; it must remain in the vine. Neither can you bear fruit unless you remain in me.
>
> I am the vine; you are the branches. If you remain in me and I in you, you will bear much fruit; apart from me you can do nothing.

The Crossroads Called Limbo

Paul is so excited about the message Jesus has placed in his heart that he's traveling far and wide to talk about Christ. At first, Christians don't trust him, and those who used to admire him are just confused. *Could this really be Saul?* But it doesn't take long to see that it's the same person. He's still on a mission. Still Type A. But this is the new version of Saul. He's even taken on a new name.

Paul has found something so life-altering in his relationship with God that he can't help but talk about it. Because of that, soon the high priests and former friends in high places realize that the old Saul isn't coming back, and that's when the second part of Ananias's message begins to unfold.

Paul is arrested, just as he once arrested others. He's placed in jail. Not the dungeon jails of the time, but under house arrest, which implies that the authorities simply don't know what to do with him. Paul is in limbo. Not totally imprisoned. But not free. He is not confined just for a few days or months, but in some instances for up to two years. During one of those long stretches, he hears the voice of Jesus again:

> That night the Lord appeared to Paul and said, "Be encouraged, Paul. Just as you have been a witness to me here in Jerusalem, you must preach the Good News in Rome as well" (Acts 23:11, *NLT*).

If the Lord Himself comes to tell you to be encouraged, chances are you're mightily discouraged, and that discouragement is understandable. Paul is on the right road. He has taken that U-turn. His old five-year-plan has been thrown out the window. Yet he keeps running into roadblocks. It's confusing! He's not in sin. He's not doing anything wrong. But he's not moving forward either, and he's burning with desire for something—anything—other than the place he's in.

Maybe you've felt that way too. Your heart is on the mend! You yearn for momentum to be visible and tangible—not just for you to experience, but for others to see. You'd love nothing more than to be able to point to those markers that say, "This is what Jesus did for me." You have a five-year-plan, but at this rate it feels like you are running a marathon at a one-mile-per-year pace.

Take comfort. You aren't the first person to feel in limbo. Something is taking place inside of you, and this limbo period might just be an important part of God's ongoing work.

> But friends, that's exactly who we are: children of God. And that's only the beginning. Who knows how we'll end up! What we know is that when Christ is openly revealed, we'll see him—and in seeing him, become like him. All of us who look forward to his Coming stay ready, with the glistening purity of Jesus' life as a model for our own (1 John 3:2-3, *THE MESSAGE*).

THE JESUS FACTOR

Paul couldn't leave his prison, so he wrote letters.

Imagine that you are Paul. Jesus Himself comes to you and tells you not to be discouraged. In response, you hold up a pile of letters. "I can't even minister. I'm in this house, sandwiched between four guards on shifts. My friends can come in, like Barnabas, but I can't go to the temple or visit people to tell them who Jesus is! Barnabas and my friends are already saved! How can I not be discouraged when You gave me a new mission, and now I'm stuck in this place?"

What Paul didn't realize was that his "limbo" period would one day be the most significant part of his ministry. Those letters he wrote became the books of Ephesians, First and Second Corinthians, Romans, Galatians, Philippians, Colossians, First and Second Thessalonians, First and Second Timothy, Titus and Philemon in the Bible. Those letters, written in limbo, didn't just influence the churches that received them while he was imprisoned at different times and places; they still impact us today. They have been translated into many different languages, read by prisoners, and held close by martyrs of the faith. They've provided comfort in hospital rooms, instructed in churches across the world and time, and challenged and changed the hearts of millions upon millions of people.

Paul knew none of that while he was in that challenging place called limbo. All he knew was that he was discouraged, and he wanted to do more.

Are you at a crossroads called limbo? Don't underestimate what God is doing in you in this season. It might very well be the most powerful place of momentum as your "letters"—the key place where God grows you and works through you—are written on your heart, and in your relationships with others.

In *Waiting on God*, John Ortberg describes waiting as "the hardest work of hope."[3] It's true. In the crossroads called limbo, we can't see down the road, or even the next step.

So, what is our response in the waiting times? It's simple: to be faithful daily.

Rather than develop a five-year or ten-year plan, or a long-term calling, we live out our call daily while we listen for God's voice. We serve faithfully as a mom. As a woman of faith. In the ordinary as we respond to what He has for us on that day, and with the people who cross our path. This doesn't mean that we can't plan, or that we don't have dreams or goals, but rather than focus on the future, we live fully in each day.

Then, as you rest in the limbo God has ordained for you, you slow down long enough to see the miracles unfolding all around you.

And in you.

That child who is snuggled against your chest just might be your greatest work in the long run. Those words of encouragement you poured over a friend's heart may bring joy where sadness once flourished. A small Sunday School class to which you show up faithfully every week can lead others closer to Christ in ways that may seem small now but produce eternal results.

If I had insisted on sticking with own my five-year plan back when I was in limbo, I would be nowhere in the vicinity of where I am today as a woman of faith. My dreams simply weren't big enough. I certainly didn't see myself as a Christian speaker. Not this shy girl who wasn't raised in church. That young mom who lay on a carpet with tears running down her face wouldn't have believed God if He had told her that one day she would speak to crowds and write books.

More importantly, I didn't know then that one day I would genuinely be free.

That freedom came out of a thousand small steps of obedience, most of which I took during the waiting or limbo time. The more I learned to lean into Him on a daily basis and simply live out my faith in the everyday elements, the more I was prepared for the bigger steps when they arrived. Not only that, I was given the gift of living my life fully in the present, rather than being fixated and frustrated over some distant time or hope.

In the crossroads called limbo, you do arrive at mile markers. You become more mature. More healed. Less surprised by or resistant to or unprepared for the good things God is giving you in the ordinary.

Your challenge is to begin to embrace the waiting times as part of the overall journey. Limbo is a key part of the healing process! As you are faithful daily, He is working in you powerfully, and it all counts.

Every single moment!

THE CROSSROADS OF HARD TIMES

Today, as my fingers rest on the keyboard, I celebrate 23 years as a cancer survivor. I wish I could have known 23 years ago that this day would come, but it was impossible to know what lay ahead.

All I had then was a fist full of fear and doctors' diagnoses.

My children were young. I was crazy in love with my husband. Life was chaotic and full and good. I was growing into God's view of me and had made peace with the past. When we received my prognosis (40% chance of surviving five years after treatment), life ground to a halt for two years as we juggled medical bills, my first major surgery, and then my second—plus chemo, radiation and endless doctor visits.

One night I stood in the bedroom, examining my changed body by the stark light of a 75-watt bulb. Rather than losing weight, I had gained. As a skinny girl, I welcomed the first 10 pounds, but not the additional 20 that followed. One breast was swollen and scarred from the segmented mastectomy. My right hand was bandaged, dark bruising peeking out around the gauze. My skin was nearly translucent, and the veins in my chest and arms were prominent from the three chemotherapy meds that had been pumped into my body to rid it of the malignant cells.

Why?

It's a question often asked in the crossroads called hard times.

It's a question Paul had every right to ask as well.

He is on his way to see Caesar in Rome when a massive storm rocks the ship. It's so frightening that the sailors and jailers all fear they will drown. Paul is in prayer. He, a lowly prisoner, runs to tell them to throw out all those things that weigh the ship down, and to hold fast to their faith. God has spoken to him. It's not going to be easy, but safety is not far away. They throw everything overboard as the ship careens into the isle of Malta, where they drag themselves ashore. Just as Paul foretold, everyone is safe.

The story gets richer. Paul is bitten by a snake; he prays and the snake falls away, dead. Paul is unharmed, and the islanders are in awe, for this is a poisonous snake. They try to worship Paul, but he sees this as a perfect opportunity to tell them about Jesus instead (see Acts 27:13–28:10,23).

It is here that Paul faces another personal crossroads. It would be easy to cast in your lot with a crowd that worships you, rather than go on to Rome where persecution, prison and likely even death await. But Paul's mission is not his own anymore. He follows where Christ leads.

They are rescued by another sailing craft, and when Paul finally arrives in Rome, he is greeted by a crowd. Now, the people who once called out his name in praise are screaming it with rage. They are kneeling in the dust and throwing the dirt toward the sky in clods as they rip at their garments (see Acts 22:23). Signs of disgust and rage.

Can you imagine? These are your former neighbors. The boys who attended temple with you. Your cousins. Those who once met with you in public, proud to be associated with you. Believers come to encourage him, but he is still surrounded by jailers, their swords lifted high around him as they march him toward Caesar. As far as Paul can see, he is in enemy territory.

At some point in your life, you will hit hard times. That's just a statistical reality. You are doing great, and then your relationship with a loved one hits a difficult patch. You choose a great church, only to be hurt by someone you thought was a friend. You are weary, or uncertain, or sick and you don't know why. You suffer a sudden financial loss or struggle. There are many hard crossroads.

When Paul was on that boat headed for the cliffs and rocks, he described the sky as being black for days and days (see Acts 27:20). Our hard crossroads can absolutely feel that way.

Yet it is in the hard times that we discover one of the most beautiful Jesus factors.

THE JESUS FACTOR

Once again Paul is writing letters. He's in limbo and hard times all at once.

I hope you never read the book of Romans in the same light again. As you do read it, place yourself beside Paul in that hard place. As you read his words, discover along with him what it means to really know Christ when there's no place else to turn.

> We can rejoice, too, when we run into problems and trials, for we know that they help us develop endurance. And endurance develops strength of character, and character strengthens our confident hope of salvation. And this hope will not lead to disappointment. For we know how dearly God loves us, because he has given us the Holy Spirit to fill our hearts with his love (Rom. 5:3-5, NLT).

Paul discovered in the crossroads of hard times that there is strength that emerges as we hold tight to Jesus' love for us. That endurance (patience, staying power) leads to an inner core of faith that is spiritually stable and stout, so that even as hard times buffet the waters around us, inside we are solidly anchored.

That day as I looked at my body—assailed by chemotherapy drugs, surgeries and radiation treatments—it wasn't a pretty sight. It was evidence of the hard times that I was going through. I didn't know what my future held, but I'll never forget standing there and raising my hands to worship my Savior in that moment. Something beautiful rose up inside of me: a sense that God was sovereign and that no matter what tomorrow held, I was a winner because I was His.

Those were scary times, and there were days when I slipped into a place of prayer just to soak in His presence because I needed it. Because I wasn't big enough to know how to fight this battle on my own. I had prepared and read, and I was doing all that I could do with knowledge and nutrition and modern medicine.

However, my hope was in Him. I even put a sign on my hospital room door:

If you don't have hope, don't come in.

My hope wasn't for the outcome, though I did pray for that. My hope was that He was with me in the midst of a storm that raged so severely that the sky was black for days and days. He was my sliver of light in that storm, and it was enough.

Your momentum isn't lost as a result of hard times or extenuating circumstances. On the contrary, they reinforce that what is taking place inside of you is greater than what comes at you from the outside.

We find not only hope in dark times, but also help.

The Holy Spirit helps us in our weakness. For example, we don't know what God wants us to pray for. But the Holy Spirit prays for us with groanings that cannot be expressed in words. And the Father who knows all hearts knows what the Spirit is saying, for the Spirit pleads for us believers in harmony with God's own will (Rom. 8:26-27, *NLT*).

When you are in hard times, Jesus speaks on your behalf, for He knows God's plan for you. When people say things like they did in Job's time—"give up" or "you must have done something wrong for this to be happening"—you can remind them that Christ suffered even though He was sinless, and He's with you in the midst of this. He knows your heart. He's standing with you, before you, behind you and over you.

When you don't have the words to express what is taking place as you pray, no words are needed, because the Holy Spirit unites your heart with God's. There is comfort in that, and also insight.

Paul discovered the greatest truth of all during hard times. It's a truth that Jesus' Church forgets far too often:

Nothing can separate us from God's love.

If you hit a hard place in your healing, and if that causes you to think you've lost every bit of your momentum, consider this:

I am convinced that nothing can ever separate us from God's love. Neither death nor life, neither angels nor demons, neither our fears for today nor our worries about tomorrow—not even the powers of hell can separate us from God's love (Rom. 8:38, *NLT*).

Paul, in his hardest moments, rested in God's secure love.

> "Jesus Christ is the same yesterday and today
> and **forever**" (Heb. 13:8). *eis ton aiona* [Greek];
> unlimited extension of time, from the past
> into the future—always, eternally, past and
> present and future.[4]

GOD AND HIS PLAN DO NOT CHANGE

Regardless of which crossroads you face, there's one principle to hold close. Write it on the mirror. In your Bible. On a Post-it note. "God and His plan for you do not change in the crossroads." Crossroads come, but they don't change God, and they don't alter His plan for you.

In the *personal* crossroads, you are asked to trust that He knows something about you and your future that you might not be able to grasp yet.

When you hit the *limbo* crossroads, you are asked to trust that He and His plan for you are unchanging, and that there are riches to be found in the waiting time.

When you hit the *hard* crossroads, you are asked to trust that this detour isn't punishment, but that you have a safe place to find comfort, hope and strength, and that you will gain endurance as a central part of your being is honed and strengthened in His loving hands.

What happens when you hold fast to this truth that God and His plan for you are unchanging in the crossroads? For some, the exterior circumstances or people around you might still look the same, but you are changed. For others, you leave behind sin or things of little value to discover the desires of your heart. For some, you scoop out of God's generous love toward you as you find renewed grace for others, and maybe even toward yourself. For others, you discover that God is your Rock.

The crossroads itself is no longer the primary message. Instead, it becomes a turning point. It is a draw-a-line-in-the-sand moment when you are growing spiritually even if others aren't willing to change. You are experiencing a deeper security in Christ when people or circumstances are unreliable.

Philip Yancey, in *The Question That Never Goes Away*, states that these places "become occasions for the work of grace, by wakening dormant reserves of courage and love and compassion that we may not have been aware of."[5]

JUST *You* AND *God*

1. How would you have described momentum before reading this chapter? How do you describe it now?

   _____

   _____

   _____

2. Which crossroads are you in right now? Which have you experienced in the past?

   _____

   _____

   _____

3. Crossroads are described as places where crucial decisions need to be made. How have you handled the decisions in the crossroads before now? Describe one way you might respond differently after reading this chapter.

   _____

   _____

   _____

4. When Paul was about to be shipwrecked, he advised the sailors to throw off everything that might weigh them down, or take the ship under water. Read Hebrews 12:1. How can throwing off unnecessary weights (sin, anger, revenge, despair, offense, and so on) assist you in the crossroads?

_____

_____

_____

_____

5. Read Isaiah 55:8-9. Have you been living with a 5-year or 10-year plan? How would living your call daily change your focus in the crossroads called limbo?

_____

_____

_____

6. Describe one miracle around you (small or large) that might be overlooked if you were focused entirely on tomorrow rather than today. Take a moment and praise God for that miracle.

_____

_____

_____

7. Read Malachi 3:6. God and His plan for you are unchanging. How does this truth affect the way you view today's crossroads?

_____

_____

_____

_____

THE MENDED HEART PRINCIPLE #7:
GOD AND HIS PLAN FOR YOU ARE UNCHANGING

There is momentum in *every* crossroads.

PRAYER

Jesus, I want so badly to run ahead of Your timing. Yet You are to be found in the personal crossroads, for there I embrace Your will over my own. In the waiting times, You grow me up and prepare me for tomorrow, but also reveal the miracles of today. In the hard times, I find You close, and You are my strength, for nothing can separate me from Your love. I invite You into my crossroads today.

MENDED HEART CHALLENGE

· Ask God to reveal the faith factor in your crossroads.
· Live fully in today, rather than with an eye on tomorrow.
· Note the miracles around you. Whether it is a loved one's smile, a kind gesture or something else, recognize God's presence in the midst of a crossroads. Take a moment and delight in it.

Notes
1. Dr. Henry Cloud, *Changes That Heal* (Grand Rapids, MI: Zondervan, 2003), p. 13.
2. "Paul's Conversion," in *IVP New Testament Commentaries*, http://www.biblegateway.com/resources/commentaries/IVP-NT/Acts/Pauls-Conversion (accessed October 2013).
3. John Ortberg, Francis Chan, et al., *Waiting on God*, Kindle version (Carol Stream, IL: Christianity Today, 2012).
4. J. P. Louw. E. A. Nida, *Greek-English Lexicon of the New Testament: Based on Semantic Domains, vol. 1*, electronic ed. of the 2nd edition (New York: United Bible Societies, 1996), # 639.
5. Philip Yancey, *The Question That Never Goes Away*, Kindle version (Brentwood, TN: Creative Trust Digital, 2013).

8

As the Heart Thinks

Imagine yourself as a living house. God comes in to rebuild that
house. . . . He is building quite a different house from the one you thought
of—throwing out a new wing here, putting on an extra floor there,
running up towers, making courtyards. You thought you were going to
be made into a decent little cottage: but He is building a palace.
He intends to come and live in it Himself.

C. S. LEWIS, *MERE CHRISTIANITY*

"So high, Gaga. We're going so high!"

Elle's tiny hands hold tight as I hold her on my lap, one arm
protectively around her waist, as we swing high on the swing.
When we arrived to visit a couple of hours earlier, she ran into
my arms, glad to see me and clearly excited about the possibility
of walking the few blocks to the playground. I believe she could
stay here all day; no matter how much fun she has had, leaving
always makes her sad.

THE PLAYGROUND OF OUR MIND

There's a playground I used to visit—one where I spent countless
hours. It was the playground of my thoughts. I went there when
someone made me angry, or when conflict arose and it hurt my

heart. I escaped there to think about all the things I should have said. I swung high, and then low, reminding myself how right I was and how wrong they were. I replayed the words or situation like a child going round and round on a merry-go-round. In this playground, I didn't have to deal with conflict in a healthy way or speak the truth when it was needed. I didn't have to admit my own errors, because in this playground I was always the hero.

One day I sensed God asking me to leave that playground. Like Elle, I wasn't ready to go, but He took me by the hand and led me away.

To a place of grace for those who said the wrong thing, reminding me that we all stumble with our words. To a place of well-being, where I recognized that conflict takes place even in the healthiest of relationships. To a place of letting go of those things that I could not change, so that I could fully embrace those that I could. There were days when I wanted to go back to my playground, but each time I approached it, I saw a "closed" sign on the gate.

Not for you, My daughter.

It was my choice. I could hop the fence if I wanted to. But my Savior was directing me back to real life. To deal with real people and real conflict, working through harder situations and growing through each one. To love the people around me, and enjoy each new day, rather than spending time devoted to thoughts that only kept me bound.

Why?

Because my God lives in me, and He desires to occupy every room. He's cleaning out old junk and debris so He can fill those places up with Himself.

Not too long ago, I talked with a friend and shared with her the long-ago story of my time in the "playground." She was quiet. Tears ran down her cheeks as we parted. To be honest,

I wondered if I had said the wrong thing. Later that week, she approached me. I sensed her joy before she said a word.

"That playground you talked about," she said. "I've been living in it constantly. In it, I think about what I wish I had, who I wish I could be, the things I would change, the words I would speak. All the time, Suzie. When you first mentioned it, I resisted the thought that this had anything to do with me. But as the week passed, I realized that there was an intense battle going on, and I am determined, with God's help, to stay out of that playground. It's changing me."

I had no idea my friend was dealing with this. Our conversation had started innocently—just two friends going deep together, sharing what we were doing, what we were writing about, what God was doing. Our ability to have these kinds of discussions is one of the things I love about our relationship.

The "playground of the mind" is not something you casually drop into the average conversation. I can only imagine someone looking at me askew, almost as if to say, "Really?" And yet it's fertile ground for many of us who have experienced hurt. That day my friend described *her* playground. She said she often drove down the street without seeing trees or a beautiful sky—because she was too focused on mentally replaying a scene or conversation over and over, rehearsing the words spoken, or words she wished she had said.

At times, she would change the real scene, re-imagining herself as the sympathetic leading actress, as everyone else acknowledged the wrongs against her.

All the while the feelings were pushing deeper, deeper, deeper.

Years ago I didn't see this as a problem. It made me feel better to tell someone what I really thought (even though they never heard the words) or to puff myself up by coming back with a zinging retort. But once God began to peel back the mask to show me what lay underneath, conviction returned any time I tried to go there.

While I viewed the playground as no big deal, Scripture says that it is. Second Corinthians 10:5 says, "We break down every thought and proud thing that puts itself up against the wisdom of God. We take hold of every thought and make it obey Christ" (*NLV*). My playground was in direct contradiction to God's plan for my thought life. It controlled me, when I should have been in control of it. It wasn't alcohol or pills, but it was just as unhealthy emotionally and spiritually.

The playground of the mind is a place where we are witty; where the offender repents; where we are respected, admired and loved; and where no one can touch us. It's living life internally. It eases pain temporarily, but it doesn't work in the long term, because we are still the same people when we check back in to real life. Our circumstances or those people or hurts haven't gone anywhere, and rather than living life fully—in the good and the bad—we have just pushed it down, buried it, or nourished the resentment and pain.

Nothing is resolved.

The playground is a stronghold. Let's break that word "stronghold" down: stranglehold, vice, iron grip, monopoly, domination, throttle. Wow, if we were to describe the way we wanted our thought life to be, none of these would seem like a pleasant option.

Neil T. Anderson, in *Freedom from Fear*, warns us that a stronghold can keep us from healing:

> Strongholds are habitual patterns of thinking, feeling, and acting that are deeply ingrained in a person's personality. They are similar in concept to what psychologists call "defense mechanisms," which are unhealthy ways of coping with life.[1]

If we begin to look at the playground as a stronghold, we see that it is an unhealthy barrier that keeps us trapped in a number of ways:

- We fail to live wholly in the moment.
- We are so focused on the past or a certain event or words that the real-life people we love receive only a portion of our attention.
- We mentally check out of a tough situation or feeling, until we can check in to the playground at a later time, which means we fail to deal with conflict, but suppress it instead.
- We fuel feelings that rob us of peace.

THE JESUS FACTOR

When I learned that I had cancer, I began to think of all the things I might want to write down for Ryan, Leslie and Melissa. Nuggets of wisdom to share with them along the way as they grew up, like: How to find the right person to love. How to be confident in who they were. How to laugh and have fun. How to be loyal to one another.

Now I understand that back then, at the age of 31, I still had much to learn myself. Wisdom would come over time, through experiences both joyful and painful, as part of a life-long journey.

Much like the journey that the disciples took with Jesus.

In Mark 8:27-34, Jesus converses with His disciples while walking along the road. As is their habit, they are talking about faith. Jesus takes every opportunity to do what I wanted to do with my children. He is pouring into His loved ones, teaching and showing them how to live. The disciples have just watched Jesus heal a blind person, as well as feed a crowd of more than 4,000 people by multiplying seven small loaves of bread (leaving seven basketfuls left over).

"Who do people say I am," He asks.

"Some say you are John the Baptist, or Elijah, or one of the prophets," they reply.

"Who do you say that I am?"

"The Messiah," Peter answers.

Jesus then explains that, as the Messiah, His destination is the cross. The disciples are aghast at this, for the cross is the cruelest death for the worst criminal. Understandably, there is confusion. Peter takes Jesus aside and scolds Him. Their entire conversation isn't recorded, so we don't know the specifics of Peter's rebuke, but consider what has just taken place. Great things are going on. People are being healed. Converts are coming into the faith. The crowd of 4,000 who just ate the bread was a mere taste of the masses that could possibly await at every port and city. Why would Jesus choose a cross and an untimely death over a booming ministry?

Jesus' response is quick and to the point. He tells Peter to "get behind" Him, saying, "You do not have in mind the concerns of God, but merely human concerns" (v. 33). In essence, He's telling Peter, "You're just thinking about you, not what God wants for *all* of humanity." This strong retort isn't founded in anger, but in the truth that comes from a heaven-down perspective.

After talking to Peter, Jesus motions to the crowd, and they gather around Him with the rest of the disciples. "Whoever wants to be my disciple must deny themselves and take up their cross and follow me," He says (v. 34).

Jesus is leading them to a profound truth.

There Is Death That Leads to Life

Perhaps you've wondered if you'll ever learn to think differently. Or if you'll ever stop reacting in a negative manner. Maybe you want your self-esteem to be based on God's view of you, rather than on your past, or on the words of another person. You're tired of letting external or old circumstances define you.

Jesus offers a new way to think. However, this transformation requires death. That's a strong word, but it clearly defines a passing away of the old so that the new can emerge. One commentary states it like this:

> The work of the Holy Ghost first begins in the understanding, and is carried on to the will, affections, and conversation, till there is a change of the whole [person] into the likeness of God, in knowledge, righteousness, and true holiness. Thus, to be godly, is to give up ourselves to God.[2]

The way that we come to think is birthed in many ways—through examples of others, experiences, pain, joy, and also through our natural temperament. Regardless of its origin, the way our heart thinks creates a distinct path that often leads us, rather than being led by us. This is where we can find ourselves in a rut. The pain is subsiding, and our heart is mending, but sometimes we create or perpetuate our own pain because of the way we think.

Margaret Thatcher once said, "Watch your thoughts, for they become words. Watch your words, for they become actions. Watch your actions, for they become habits. Watch your habits, for they become your character. And watch your character, for it becomes your destiny!"

When we begin to understand the power of our thoughts, we have an opportunity to create a new groove in our thought patterns, which creates a new way of looking at life and others. This in turn changes the way we respond and act. Over time, our new behaviors become natural and ingrained in our character, which leads us in a whole different direction in any number of areas.

When I was in that playground described earlier, it felt good, but my thoughts could lead me to stagnate rather than to grow. They could lead me to act out, become defensive or bitter, build walls, or form a worldview that limited my choices and poisoned my attitude. They could absolutely lead me to isolate, as I became my own best friend—because who else would treat me so well? Understanding this progression allowed me to view my thought life differently. To see that playground as a means by which my heart was being shaped. To recognize how it was affecting my loved ones, my outlook and me. When I sensed God asking me to shut down my unhealthy thoughts, it was because God had more for me.

God also has more for you.

Change is ahead for all of us; we were never intended to live in a stagnant state. Each of us was created to explore all that God has for us—to build a faith-filled bucket list that challenges us to push beyond obstacles and limitations to see what is on the other side.

In Proverbs 23:7, Solomon says, "For as he thinketh in his heart, so is he" (*KJV*). Consider that for a moment. Really hold up your thought life to the examination of the Holy Spirit.

- Where do you most often spend your time in your thought life?
- Where does your thought life lead you?
- How does it impact those you love?

- What does it offer you? (There must be benefits, or we wouldn't hold on to it.)
- Is there negative feedback (from those who love you most, or even in your own response to it) that you have ignored?
- What might God want to offer you instead?

For as you think in your heart, so are you.

When this challenge presents itself, our first instinct may be to scold our Savior, like Peter did. It doesn't feel good. We love the fruits and the gifts of our faith, but when we are asked to join in with Him in change, it's easier to point out that others need to be fixed, or to just stay where we are.

But our Savior comes to us with both grace and truth (see John 1:14).

Grace gives us what we need right where we are, and so much more that we may not deserve. It's the compassionate character of God that is relational—that communes with and loves His own. But He also holds out truth. It's just as much a gift, for it's a very personal view of what you can do, and where to go next.

Imagine a child carrying a heavy load upon her shoulders. There's a place to lay her burden down, but she carries it everywhere she goes. Grace and empathy make you want to reach out and take that heavy pack from her stooped shoulders. You see the exhaustion the weight is causing. You watch as she occasionally stops to pick up another stone or boulder and place it on top of the other weights. You see the damage being done to her tiny bones, and you note the refusal that comes repeatedly as she rejects your offers of help. You aren't condemning her for carrying that weight. You care for her and want to remove it!

Truth takes your offer of help to a new level. It's no longer a gentle suggestion; it's a clear call for the burden-carrying girl to put the weight down. It's not cloaked or vague. It reveals the stooped shoulders in the mirror. It reveals the stubbornness that keeps on packing the burden, even as there is a place to put it down.

> Come to me, all you who are weary and burdened, and I will give you rest. Take my yoke upon you and learn from me, for I am gentle and humble in heart, and you will find rest for your souls. For my yoke is easy and my burden is light (Matt. 11:28-30).

Emily Freeman, in *A Million Little Ways*, calls this rest a "joyful release." She says:

> We are all walking our own dusty roads. None of us are exempt from the prerequisites of a joyful release—death, surrender, brokenness, and humility. But the cross is beautiful because those heavy companions do not come alone. We do not have to bear their weight.
>
> God left a love-trail through history, and it all points to the resurrection. And even though death precedes new life, love came first to pave the way. Love is the invisible hand of God made visible on the cross, in the tomb, through the resurrection.
>
> And now his love is made visible through us, through the deepest desires of believers, through image bearers waking up in the presence of God.[3]

Where do we begin as we prepare for this joyful release?

DENY YOURSELF

Strangely enough, we can find great joy in denying ourselves. This idea may be hard to grasp, for it goes against the grain of our cultural thinking. The invitation to deny ourselves is a big swing from 100 percent living in our own strengths or going with our feelings.

Instead it's forming a kinship with Christ. You are still uniquely you, but you begin to understand that destructive or unhealthy feelings, reactive responses and choices, and ingrained habits and behaviors aren't going to be your go-to options anymore. In a close-knit relationship with Him, you walk in the opposite direction from the harmful influences of your past, for in self-denial you receive a "renewed mind."

> Therefore, I urge you, brothers and sisters, in view of God's mercy, to offer your bodies as a living sacrifice, holy and pleasing to God—this is your true and proper worship. Do not conform to the pattern of this world, but be transformed by the renewing of your mind. Then you will be able to test and approve what God's will is— his good, pleasing and perfect will (Rom. 12:1-2).

I love that Paul describes this as worship. Denying yourself means that you lift your heart to Him to surrender what once defined you and to accept what He knows you can be. Denying yourself leads to carrying the cross. That's when we stand before our heavenly Father and give all of ourselves—all that we are, all that we once were, all that we can do, and all that we want to be.

Our Christian faith calls this process "conversion" or "sanctification," which simply means that a holy change is taking place inside of your soul. One that will go on for the rest of your days. On the *Ekklesia Project* blog, Kyle Childress writes,

"Following Jesus and the way of the cross begins with small steps. Later, we'll look up and discover where he's led us."[4]

FEEL, FELT, FOUND

It won't be easy at first; often we don't recognize how strong a hold a certain behavior or thought pattern has on us until we try to let go of it. But change comes over time as the Holy Spirit clearly defines pivotal moments for us, and we partner with Christ in stepping into them.

Years after that moment of conviction when God asked me to leave the playground, I was on a very long drive. I was returning home after traveling to another state to help a friend after surgery. Before I left, she had asked me to check her emails and to print them out for her to read, specifically requesting that I read through them and throw away any spam.

As I scanned several emails, one stood out. I wasn't sure what to do with it. Should I delete it? Give it to her and expose her secret? I sat at her desk, the printed email in my hand, hurt and angry.

When she had asked me to help her after the surgery, I knew that it might be difficult. This friend was estranged from members of her family and struggled with addiction. Her request was sincere. She needed help. I knew it was something that I was privileged to be able to do.

The email, however, reflected a very different sentiment from anything she had expressed to me. It was a response from a stranger she had been conversing with over the Internet. Her prior message had explained that I was on my way, and then painted me in terms that hurt my heart. They were not borderline untrue, but blatantly false.

In effect, she said, "I have to put up with her because I have no one else."

His response was, "Poor baby. So sorry you have to put up with such a @&%."

I was hurt on many levels and for many reasons. Because my friend had misrepresented my character. Because the words were said to some strange man who didn't even know me. Because she had begged me to come, and the trip was inconvenient and costly on my part. Because I had done what she asked, with good intentions. I was reading these words after I had loved her, sat with her, fed her, washed her clothes, cleaned up after her sickest moments, changed her bedding, watched her children, fed her dogs, and prayed with her.

Do you see where this is going?

I hadn't told her about the email. I simply deleted it. But as I drove home, I dove into that playground to make my case. For well over three hours, as I drove down the busy interstate, I thought:

I did [fill in the blank] for you.
Why would you say such hurtful things?
Don't you realize this is why people walk away from you?

I imagined all the things I thought she should hear. I defended myself. I envisioned what it might have been like if she had been forced to fend for herself. While I understood that her words had come from a broken place inside of her, and that the root of her brokenness had nothing to do with me, it didn't make me feel any better.

But the playground did.

Then I sensed it all over again: my Savior taking me by the hand, leading me out of the playground to a healthier place.

It's not for you, Suzie. Not today. Not tomorrow. Not ever.

Tears ran down my cheeks as He led me to pray for her, and to hand Him my own burden of sadness. It was a mandate to not let my disappointment become a vice-like grip on my heart, and to stop laboring to mentally reformat and reframe things that were beyond my power. He wasn't asking me to pretend not to feel, or to dismiss the way my friend's words made me feel, but to give it the proper room in my thoughts—and thus in my heart.

It was also an invitation to step back mentally and unpack the situation. In this instance, I was dealing with someone who lashed out as a result of her own pain and stung those closest to her. I knew my motivation. I knew my own heart and character. So why would I take words that were untrue and allow them to cause me pain? I also knew the pattern of behavior that had pushed others away.

Most importantly, I knew beyond a doubt that God had led me there.

Did He promise that it would be easy? No.

Did He say that it would all work out well in the end? No, He didn't.

I believe that my heavenly Father asked me to do this particular task because my friend matters to Him. In helping her after her surgery, I got to experience the God who sees the sparrow fall, who knows the number of hairs on our head, and who says, "If God cares so wonderfully for flowers that are here today and thrown into the fire tomorrow, he will certainly care for you" (Luke 12:28). In this case, He was caring for my friend's very personal and intimate needs and trusting that I would partner with Him in the assignment. Rather than take her brokenness personally, I had an opportunity to redirect my thoughts to the beauty of a Savior who could fill those hurting places—in both of us.

Unpacking the situation completely changed my attitude and my response to the hurtful email. Your unpacking may show you that there is a need for healthy boundaries. It may lead to a response of, "this is not okay" as you share your needs in a relationship or situation. Maybe it's necessary that you work things out together, if that's possible. Sometimes as I've unpacked my response, there has been truth waiting to be discovered—just enough truth (even if it wasn't presented in the right way) that I give myself grace to grow, but I do not give it power to keep me chained to the words or person.

Another friend of mine, Luann Prater, describes this process like this: feel, felt, found.

You feel it.

You don't pretend that your emotional response doesn't exist, because it does. You give yourself a moment to acknowledge that it hurts, that it's unfair, that it's not okay.

You felt it.

Do you remember a previous time when you felt this way? What did you learn from that? How did it teach you? Did you grow through it? How did God meet that need at that time?

You found.

What did you discover in that earlier experience? What did the bigger picture look like (in hindsight)? What did you see afterwards that you couldn't see in the heat of emotion? If you were talking to a friend who was going through the same situation, what would you say you found (discovered, uncovered, realized), and what advice would you give your friend?

Once we "feel, felt, found," we grab hold of the truth that Jesus also went through experiences that were hurtful, trials that seemed too big, and pain that came when He did the right thing and suffered anyway. Hebrews 2:16-18 puts it like this:

> It's obvious, of course, that he didn't go to all this
> trouble for angels. It was for people like us, children
> of Abraham. That's why he had to enter into every

detail of human life. Then, when he came before God as high priest to get rid of the people's sins, he would have already experienced it all himself—all the pain, all the testing—and would be able to help where help was needed (*THE MESSAGE*).

The process of renewing your thinking is purposeful. It requires recognizing when you are slipping into old patterns, and then shutting the gate rather than running into that playground.

You may put a thought down, only to pick it back up moments later. Or you might want to "go there" so badly that it's literally a spiritual battle. I discovered that the battle becomes less fierce as we continue to deny ourselves in this area. Then one day we recognize those thoughts for what they are. Strongholds. Vice grip. Stranglehold. Throttle. From that point forward, we don't want them anymore. They hold no appeal. We have firmly shut the gate to the unhealthy playground in our mind, freeing ourselves to live fully.

When you shut the gate to the unhealthy playground in your mind, it frees you to live in today. No matter what your past held. No matter how hard things might have been at one time, or what another broken person might say to you that is untrue or unfair.

SHUTTING THE GATE

ennoia [Greek]; consideration, **thought**, attitude. *nous* [Greek]; mind.

Shutting the gate to the playground of your mind opens the door to a spiritual makeover.

Renewal in your thinking leads you to a place of maturity where you consider how your thoughts influence you. It's a deliberate approach that allows you to give conflict and broken people and hurtful words their rightful place. You stop expending great amounts of energy and your heart on things you cannot change, so that you can put that same energy into those things that you can.

Rather than carrying a heavy personal load around with you all the time, you unpack that load so you can deal with and work through it. You get rid of those things that aren't your burden to shoulder.

Your thoughts become a sacred place that Jesus has renovated, restored and reclaimed as His own.

JUST *You* AND *God*

1. In the *Amplified Bible*, 1 John 4:4 reads: "Little children, you are of God [you belong to Him] and have [already] defeated and overcome them [the agents of the antichrist], because He Who lives in you is greater (mightier) than he who is in the world." A playground is somewhere we love to spend time in and might struggle to leave. How does Jesus help you move from the "playground of your mind" to a renewed mind?

   _____
   _____
   _____
   _____
   _____
   _____
   _____
   _____

2. List the reasons you might resist leaving your old ways of thinking. What do you gain by staying (there's always a reward)? What do you lose?

_____

_____

_____

_____

3. Solomon says, "As you think in your heart, so are you." Hold up your thought life and examine it. Where has it led you? Where would you like it to lead you instead? Make that a prayer.

_____

_____

_____

_____

4. Margaret Thatcher said that thoughts become actions, which become habits, which become your destiny. How have your old ways of thinking delayed your healing?

_____

_____

_____

_____

5. As you deny yourself in this area, it will certainly change you, but it will likely have a broader effect as well. How might your transformation impact others who you care about?

_____

_____

_____

_____

6. Consider a thought that is unhealthy. Use the *feel, felt, found* process.

    a. How does it make you feel?
    b. Was there another time when you felt this same way?
    c. In hindsight, is there something you learned from that?
    d. How can that insight help you today?

_____
_____
_____
_____

5. Your thoughts are a sacred place where God wants to create renewed spaces to fill with His presence. You have a role in this process as well:

    a. *Empty it* (see Phil. 4:6). What is one thing that you will place at the foot of the Cross today?
    b. *Replace it* (see Phil. 4:8). What is one attribute you desire in place of the thing you are releasing?
    c. *Invite your Best Friend to move in* (see Phil. 4:13). In what ways will God do the heavy lifting in this process?

_____
_____
_____
_____

The Mended Heart Principle #8:
As Your Heart Thinks, So Are You

Your thoughts are a place where God wants to live.

Prayer

Dear Jesus, I have spent hours in my thoughts where I am angry, or I am the hero, or I tell someone what I should have said, or I put them in their place. Today I recognize all of that as a trap of the enemy. Today, with Your help, I shut the gate to the playground of unhealthy thoughts. I put them down; when I start to pick them up again, remind me that they are a burden, and that You have more for me than this.

Mended Heart Challenge

- Prayerfully go on a "thought" fast. Anytime an unhealthy thought comes to mind, deny it. Do not entertain it. Do not nurture it.
- Do this for one week.
- Fill your thoughts with one Scripture each day (2 Tim. 1:7 is a great one to begin with). Place the verse where you will see it several times throughout the day. Read it out loud.

Notes
1. Neil T. Anderson, *Freedom from Fear* (Eugene, OR: Harvest House Publishers, 1999), p. 35.
2. "Romans 12," in *Matthew Henry's Concise Commentary*. http://www.christnotes.org/commentary.php?b=45&c=12&com=mhc (accessed October 2013).
3. Emily P. Freeman, *A Million Little Ways* (Grand Rapids, MI: Revell, 2013), p. 55.
4. Kyle Childress, "Following Jesus One Step at a Time," *Ekklesia Project*, February 29, 2012. http://www.ekklesiaproject.org/blog/2012/02/following-jesus-one-step-at-a-time/ (accessed October 2013).

9

Moving Toward Joy

One can never consent to creep when one feels an impulse to soar.

HELEN KELLER, *THE STORY OF MY LIFE*

According to some estimates, I made 5,000 decisions today.
Seriously?

Well, I made a decision to get out of bed. I made a choice to put on my tennis shoes and walk. I chose a green smoothie over sugared cereal. I weighed which bills to pay. What to make for dinner. Whether to answer a phone call. Which clothes to wear. Whether the plants needed watering or if they could wait another day. I chose to fill up the Prius instead of the gas-guzzler.

Wait! I may have made *more* than 5,000 decisions today!

THE MATH OF CHOICES

It seems like it was just yesterday that I was that young mom, or the teenaged girl going to the little community college. I remember what it felt like to be pregnant with my babies, and how I felt when they each stood at the altar to wed the person they loved. I'm now watching my parents and in-laws grow old. More and more of my peers have lost one or both of their parents, so I treasure my time with mine.

My beautiful mom struggles to breathe when she walks very far, and her eyesight is failing. My dad is wiry and strong, but he winces in pain due to an old injury. Each of these things reminds me that time is adding up—minute by minute, year by year, decade by decade.

The longer I am on this earth, the more I see how the seemingly smallest of choices can be the most important. These tiny decisions play into longevity, relationships, career or ministry, and more. Yet we may not give our smaller choices the respect they deserve. We only see *now*. How we feel right at this second. What might happen in the next five minutes. This right-now mentality can cause us to fail to weigh the long-term results of countless choices along the way, such as:

- How we react or respond to a loved one.
- Whether or not we create drama with someone who has hurt our feelings.
- Whether we spend time with our heavenly Father or push that time to another day.
- Whether we say those words that will cause another person pain.

With our 5,000 choices each day, we are actively carving out relationships and leaving an imprint that says, "I was here." What might happen if we could stand on the tallest mountain and look back at the culmination of each of our choices? Even as I write this, the scope of that prospect is sobering.

A couple of years ago, I was on a ministry trip in Europe. I've worked with this team three times, so I'm not unaware of the intense travel schedule, but this trip was especially brutal. We were traveling to three countries in 12 days and ministering up to three times a day. We were exhausted. One night, we just

missed our train. The coordinator who was with us had accident-
ly read the schedule wrong. Wheeling heavy bags behind us, we
raced to catch the train . . . but it was too late, and the next train
wasn't leaving for a long time. There we stood on the platform
in the moonlight. It was nearing midnight and our destination
was two hours away. The weather was cold and wet. We had a
ministry event scheduled early the next morning. We were looking at three hours of sleep at the most.

The coordinator walked over to our team. "I'm so sorry," she
said. "I didn't mean for it to work out this way."

There we all stood at a choice point. But I wasn't responsible
for anyone's response but my own. I could express my frustration. I could explain that my sleep tank was on empty. I could
choose to say nothing while sighing with a martyred expression.
In those few short seconds (which is normally the amount of
time we have with a choice point), I reminded myself what a
privilege it is to be in ministry. Ease and comfort were never
offered to our Savior, and losing a little sleep was nothing in
comparison. I reminded myself that everyone around me was
just as tired as I was.

Plus I was in Europe, for pete's sake.

"I'm good," I said, "In fact, it's been an amazing day and I
can't wait to see what God does tomorrow."

The coordinator grabbed me and pulled me into a huge hug.
"Thank you, Suz."

She was just as exhausted as I was, and my response, while
it didn't make the train arrive any sooner, lifted a weight from
her shoulders.

I wish I could say that I handle every choice point in this
same way, but sometimes I fail. Maybe it's that moment when
someone is talking about another person and I listen in.

I'm not the one gossiping, so it's not a problem.

Or the time I am hurt, and I know just the words to say to make me look like I'm "right," while allowing the other person to feel the brunt of my frustration. I can couch it in terms that sound polite, even. It's a verbal whipping with soft words, but the heart behind it is payback.

They deserved that.

In those failures, I am reminded that over time, the math of choice points doesn't just add up—it multiplies. Our choices affect those within the vicinity of our decisions, throwing them into choice points of their own—which in turn affect more people.

What does this have to do with brokenness?

When we acknowledge that we have been harmed by another's choices, we don't have to sign up to keep that cycle going. I treasure the knowledge that my heavenly Father offers grace and unconditional love. I hold fast to the foundation of rest in what has already been done for me. But I also partner in the healing process, as well as change how I choose to go forward.

We make our choices, but then our choices make us. An anonymous writer once said, "The most important thing in life is knowing the most important things in life."

A kind word. A patient response. Waiting to have all the facts rather than lashing out. These may seem like little things, but the choices we make echo the inner workings of our hearts. Our hope is that those choices change over time, coming to more closely resemble the "new creation" we are becoming.

OUR CHOICES LEAVE A LEGACY

What is the difference between a choice point and a crossroads? Our crossroads are usually bigger, more obvious choices. We often carefully consider them because we recognize their importance. Even if they don't cause us to pause in the beginning, over time they grab our attention. However, our everyday choices come and go quickly, and their significance varies greatly. Some are random, others weighty. Most are seemingly insignificant decisions, but they add up over time, nestled in the 5,000 decisions we make every day.

Shauna Niequist, in her book *Cold Tangerines*, says:

> I want a life that sizzles and pops and makes me laugh out loud. And I don't want to get to the end, or to tomorrow, even, and realize that my life is a collection of meetings and pop cans and errands and receipts and dirty dishes. I want to eat cold tangerines and sing loud in the car with the windows open and wear pink shoes and stay up all night laughing and paint my walls the exact color of the sky right now. I want to sleep hard on clean white sheets and throw parties and eat ripe tomatoes and read books so good they make me jump up and down and I want my everyday to make God belly laugh, glad that he gave life to someone who loves the gift.[1]

As you read this, can't you picture the joy? It's not that Shauna isn't also awash in laundry and the daily duties of motherhood. It's not that she doesn't have to drive through a crush of traffic. It certainly isn't that she hasn't experienced brokenness, for that is part of her testimony. In her own words, she has chosen to "believe that there is nothing more sacred or profound than this day."[2]

We intentionally move toward joy as we see each day—including *this* day—as sacred.

Life isn't static. It's constantly moving. So too are our opportunities for choices. How do you choose to see this day, with all of its good and hard moments, as sacred (i.e., blessed, holy, consecrated, set apart to honor God)? How do you live in this way when you've suffered loss, or had a messed-up childhood, or find yourself in a relationship gone bad?

Ann Voskamp, in *One Thousand Gifts*, says, "The secret to joy is to keep seeking God where we doubt He is."[3]

Hear my heart. I am a cancer survivor. I grew up in a dysfunctional and often abusive environment. I've faced financial hardships that have brought my husband and me to our knees. My biological father raped my mom, and that's a heritage I'm not excited about. I don't share these intimate details to say, "Look at me," but rather to acknowledge that there are things that can move us toward sadness, or that are not fair, or that leave a mark. Those factors, if we hold the past more sacred than today, can absolutely affect our choices.

We lash out and say, "That's just who I am. Deal with it."

We blame another person's example. "It's all I've ever known. It's her fault."

We run in the opposite direction of God. "Where was He when I needed Him?"

These are our yesterdays.

If you hold each day sacred, you live in today—not in your past. You do so understanding that today will contain many choices and perhaps some hardships. But it will also hold out those things that make your heart happy, if you tune in to them.

Steve Jobs once said, "Remembering that I'll be dead soon is the most important tool I've ever encountered to help me make the big choices in life."[4] It almost seems intrusive to peek into this very private statement, but in the last days of his sickness, this successful, busy man—who wasn't always celebrated for his personal choices or attitudes toward people—discovered that his greatest choices didn't have a lot to do with success or business or getting ahead, but were actually those that had seemed the smallest until he held just a remnant of days in his hands.

It's true that of the 5,000 choices we make each day, there are some that truly don't matter, like which way the toilet paper is placed on the roll. (And yet how much attention and energy do we give things like that?!) But many that seem insignificant in the moment will have great meaning in days to come.

Which choices will become your choice-point carbon footprint?

Whatever you decide, that will be your legacy.

THE JESUS FACTOR

When we look at Jesus' life, we see a wide variety of decisions. There were times when He stopped to heal someone, even if it was inconvenient; at other times, He passed by immediate needs in order to pursue His overall mission. Sometimes He was patient, and other times stern. There were clear-cut commandments like "love one another as I have loved you" and "love the Lord your God with all your heart, soul and mind," and then there were parables that left the disciples scratching their heads.

It wasn't that He was inconsistent, by any means, for there were foundational principles that undergirded everything He did. It was just that each choice point held its own variables.

One absolute consistency is that Jesus relied on the Holy Spirit to lead Him. Several times throughout Scripture, when the disciples were uncertain, or when they needed assurance that they wouldn't make completely wrong decisions, He encouraged them with truths such as this:

But when he, the Spirit of truth, comes, he will guide you into all the truth. He will not speak on his own; he will speak only what he hears, and he will tell you what is yet to come. He will glorify me because it is from me that he will receive what he will make known to you (John 16:13-14).

Jesus was introducing them to a Helper. A Counselor. An Advocate.

> **Spirit of Truth. Counselor.**
> **Advocate (names of the Holy Spirit):**
> One who intercedes on behalf of another.
> A helper.

HELP WITH FAITH CHOICE POINTS

Throughout the book of Exodus, we find the Spirit, like a pillar of fire or a pillar of cloud, leading the people of Israel as they carried the Ark of the Covenant to their new homeland (see, for example, Exod. 13:21). We see Moses sitting in the Tent of Meeting, the glory of God settling over that humble temple as He and Moses talked (see Exod. 33:9). In the days of King Solomon, the Temple was designed to be a dwelling place for God's Spirit. Though every temple was not always a habitation for God's presence (perhaps because a priest or people were in sin), when it was, the glory of God was described as a glorious light or cloud. This represents the *Schechinah* (הניכש) presence of God, which dwelled or settled among His people, who always observed it in wonder and awe (see Exod. 33:10).

When Jesus came, His mission changed all of that. There was a new temple for the Spirit of God. This new temple is made of living believers. Rather than standing at a distance, watching others experience God, we each have the Holy Spirit living inside of us (see Rom. 5:5; 8:9,11; 1 John 3:24).

Which is an awe factor of our faith, and a gift that is not celebrated enough.

Shifting God's Spirit from a physical building or a series of rituals to our own hearts offers us close access to Jesus. The Holy Spirit knows God's intentions for us. He sees the bigger picture. He also knows the heart of the person on the other end of each of our choice points. Thus Jesus' mission takes an intimate turn. Not only does He open our eyes, bring good news to the poor, deliver the oppressed, and heal the brokenhearted, but He also does all of that from the inside out.

Christ is as close as your own heartbeat.

You now have a Helper in your choice points as the Holy Spirit helps you seek truth and act accordingly (see 1 Cor. 2:10-11). This removes the focus from rules or even a blueprint, and places it on the Spirit who lives inside of you. Which is handy, for choices are not always clear. Scripture doesn't lay every possible option out in black and white. As a rule follower, I have definitely faced situations where I would have loved nothing more than a handbook that spelled it all out. Then again, the Pharisees and Sadducees had exactly that, and it didn't work out very well for them.

HELP IN YOUR CHOICE POINTS WITH OTHERS

That same Helper or Advocate is there to help you in your choice points that involve or impact others.

Not too long ago, I was in an airport, waiting out weather-related delays. My city had sunny skies, but our destination did not. Delay one came. Delay two. Then delay three. People were making choices all around me, and some of them were poor ones. I'm used to delays, so I was looking ahead—trying to figure out how I was going to manage L.A. traffic in a rental car after dark. Even if I made it out of the next airport, which was experiencing cancellations ahead of an impending blizzard, I would be landing in California hours later than originally planned.

I was engrossed in a telephone conversation with an airline employee when a woman started shouting. I had noticed her earlier. She had gone to the bar during each delay, and it was catching up with her. She was angry and was letting all those around her know it. It wasn't her actions that surprised me, however. It was those of other, already irritated passengers. Some began to say things, like *Shut up! Sit down and be quiet! You're going to get kicked out of the airport, lady.*

"Stop shouting," one man shouted.

The woman retreated to her seat.

Selfishly, I began to wonder what this would mean for our flight. The Boston Marathon bombing had taken place the weekend before, and every airline was on high alert. Would this woman make it onto the plane? Would she make a scene if she did? Would we have to turn around?

That's when I felt a nudge from the Holy Spirit, who lives inside of me. After years of loving Jesus, I recognize His direction. It's insistent. Not a whim, but an assignment. I paused to see if the impression persisted. My heart beat a little faster as I realized that God was indeed asking something of me.

I sat beside the woman. "Where are you headed?" I asked.

She looked up, her hair falling over one eye. She squinted and said, "Who are you, and why are you in my face?"

These words were not what I had hoped I would hear. Sometimes the choices we make with people are not perfectly tied up in a neat, magical bow. We might not instantly see the fruit that comes from those choice points. Or, as in this instance, we may initially see negative fruit that makes us question *why*. I tried again. "It seems like you are having a really bad day. It's a bummer to be delayed." (I know. So eloquent, right?)

"I'm going to a funeral."

And then it all came spilling out. She had been raised in a bad home and was neglected. Someone finally alerted the authorities, and the state picked her up and took her to a safe place. The only problem was that for the next few years, her safe place became her nightmare. She was molested over and over. "That's when she rescued me," she said.

An aunt who lived hundreds of miles away finally located her and stepped in to be her guardian. At the age of 14, this young girl finally had a home where she was cared for, loved and protected.

"She was a prayer warrior," she said. "Do you know what that is?"

I nodded.

"She prayed for me all the time, even when I messed up. She was all I had."

Her aunt had been murdered a day earlier, and suddenly the only person who had ever loved this woman was gone. It was apparent that she didn't fly much. The ticket had cost her a great deal because it was a last-minute reservation, and she was afraid the delays would cause her to miss the funeral. Alcohol had served as her only consolation.

And the people around her had become bullies.

"May I pray with you?" I asked.

She cried as we prayed together.

My Advocate helped me to know what to say, and what not to say. It was a simple prayer, asking God to comfort her and help her in a hard time.

"Do you think that she is looking down from heaven and sent you to me?" she asked.

"I think God saw you," I said, "and wanted you to not be alone."

There were no assigned seats on this airline, so she ended up sitting next to me on the plane. We talked about kids and grandkids. Sometimes she slept. Other times she got loud, especially when the flight attendant turned down her request for a drink. She joked that we were "kicking [cute] grannies" and I took it for the compliment she intended. We parted in Denver with a hug.

I don't get to see the end of this story, at least not this side of heaven. All I know is that I got to play a small part in it.

Why did God choose me for that assignment? I'm not sure. Perhaps it's because there's alcoholism in my family tree, and it's something that I can see past. I'm not afraid of it, and I know how to deal with it. (Isn't it amazing how God can use the painful aspects of our past in beautiful and surprising ways?)

Regardless of the reason, you and I have the opportunity every day to impact others with our choices. It may not be a big assignment; it may be something as minor as smiling instead of scowling at a stranger, or toning down our road rage to enjoy the ride. It may be giving sacrificially instead of holding on to what is ours. No matter the choice point, we can move toward joy as we take the opportunity to discover our part in Jesus' love for others. This isn't a Pollyannaish way of looking at life. It's living within the bigger picture, as we learn to listen and respond to the Holy Spirit within us.

Now, this is the part that makes me want to put on my dancing shoes.

As you mend, you will discover that you move from needing help to giving it. God will use your story, with the help of the Advocate, to come alongside those who are still a work in progress.

They may be traveling down a road you recognize but are no longer on. You understand their challenges. You see through the defense mechanisms and excuses, but you also identify with the deep need.

You know in which direction to point in order to help them find hope.

CHOICE POINTS WITH LOVED ONES

In *The Unburdened Heart*, I describe some of the choices we make with loved ones:

- How many times do we choose to hold a grudge instead of to forgive?
- How many times do we gossip about someone instead of giving her grace?
- How many times do we say those things that we know pierce the heart of a person because we are angry or tired or frustrated, or just plain ol' irritated? Especially with the people we love the best. They are the easiest to treat disrespectfully, because they love us. They'll accept our apology, right?[5]

A mended heart is one that moves intentionally toward joy. Another word for joy is happiness. Whether or not we are happy does affect those we love the most.

But what if happiness seems like a distant and unreachable target?

Let's begin by defining the term. Happiness is not having a lot of nice things. It's not being at your optimum weight. It's not success. It's not even having a life free of problems. It is deep peace, an underlying state of satisfaction, an attitude or state of being in harmony with life and at peace with God.

Leslie Vernick is a licensed professional family therapist, author and speaker. My friend Luann Prater and I host a radio show, and we interviewed Leslie about a book she had written, titled *Lord, I Want to Be Happy*.[6] In her book, Vernick defines happiness as one of our most powerful choice points with our loved ones. She takes it further, saying that regardless of our temperaments or situations, we can learn to be happy.

This begins as we stop identifying ourselves by our feelings. Rather than saying, "I'm sad" or "I'm angry," she asks that we take ownership by saying, "I'm feeling sad" or "I'm feeling angry" instead. Then the logical next step becomes:

- What is making me feel sad, and how can I address that?
- What is making me feel angry, and what will my response be?

The first benefit to this approach is that it allows us to address the real issue, rather than getting tangled in the emotion.

Second, we remove the other person from the equation. It's not, "*She's* making me sad," but rather, "I need to feel appreciated from time to time."

Or we replace "*He's* the worst ex-husband ever" with "It hurts when something I wanted to work didn't."

Reframing our emotional response in this way instantly offers a realistic glimpse of the need inside.

You might ask, "What if pinpointing the need only shows me what I might never receive?" This is a hard but fair question.

The key to experiencing true healing is to stop trying to fill up with what someone else might not have to give. If it's a broken parent who will never say those words you wish you could hear, you hold close the words Jesus has spoken over you. You befriend a godly older woman who sees the value in you. You speak the words you long to hear over others, for you know the power contained within them.

If it's an ex who has gone his or her own way, you find comfort in a God who says He'll never leave or forsake you. You pore over the Scriptures that remind you that you are beloved and worthy. You forgive so that you can move on with what God has for you—for God and His plans for you do not change, even if things didn't work out as you had hoped.

Taking these steps allows you to receive a spiritual and emotional dividend. You are able to look at those people who *are* speaking kind words to you, who *do* encourage you or love you, and stop asking them to pay the price for what someone else has failed to do.

GRATITUDE THERAPY

What about those days when it seems impossible to choose happiness?

You choose gratitude instead. In our interview with Vernick, she described being at church one morning. A family with several small children sat behind her. Except they didn't sit. They pushed on the back of the pew. They ran up and down the length of the pew. They were noisy and distracting. Leslie strained to listen to the pastor, and the longer this went on, the more irritated she began to feel. Remember, she wasn't angry. She wasn't irritated.

She was *feeling* irritable. She was *feeling* angry.

She closed her eyes and began engaging in a little gratitude therapy.

> *Thank You, God, that this young family is in church. It must have been so hard for them to make it here with these little ones. Thank You, God, that I can be here, worshiping You with others.*

Thank You, God, for parents who try so hard to teach their children about You. For if this is exhausting for me, how much harder it must be for this young mom and dad.

This exercise completely shifted Vernick's perspective from "I'm feeling angry" to one of appreciation, which flipped her attitude upside down.

What might happen in our choice points with our loved ones if we did the same?

Not too long after the interview, I had an opportunity to practice Vernick's method. I was *feeling* frustrated and *feeling* angry after an awkward and unsettling encounter with a loved one. I started to silently thank God for this person. I began listing the qualities that I loved. This brought up an image of a time when this person had done something that made me so joy-filled. That led me to thank God for other little things, which had nothing to do with the encounter or the person.

Like the beautiful day outside. Dinner simmering on the stove. The butterfly bush outside my front door that was blooming with purple, fragrant flowers.

I was blown away by the change in my emotions. Frustration ebbed. Anger sizzled out. Yes, we had some stuff to work through and it wasn't fun, but I could now do that without the super-charged feelings.

Now the resolution was wrapped in gratitude, and the outcome had an opportunity to look different. Gratitude therapy equipped me to do to others "as [I] wish[ed] that others would do to [me]" (Luke 6:31, *ESV*).

JUST *You* AND *God*

1. We started in Chapter One with "what you don't have to do." Why might it be healing to look at "what you can do"?

_____

_____

_____

2. Happiness comes not by passive waiting, but by active participation. What are your thoughts on this statement?

_____

_____

_____

3. John 16:13 says that "when he, the Spirit of truth, comes, he will guide you into all the truth." This Spirit of truth lives inside of you. In what ways do you desire this Helper or Advocate to help you in your choice points?

_____

_____

_____

_____

4. Before today you may have described yourself by your emotions: *I'm sad. I'm bitter. I'm furious.* Write down the emotions you are feeling. Change the statements from "I'm [fill in the blank]" to "I'm feeling [fill in the blank]." How does doing this change the way you look at this emotion?

_____

_____

_____

_____

5. Now it's time to look at the real issue beneath that feeling. Rather than focusing on another person's actions, qualities or inabilities, consider what it is that you really need. Finish this sentence: *What I need is . . .*

_____

_____

_____

_____

6. Go to the core of the actual need. How can God fill this need?

_____

_____

_____

_____

7. Are there other ways that this need can be addressed in spiritual and healthy ways (licensed Christian counseling, godly mentoring, helping others, taking a class or learning coping tools, filling up with joy in other spiritual ways, and so on)?

_____

_____

_____

_____

8. Read 1 Thessalonians 5:18. Take a moment to practice gratitude therapy. Consider a recent conflict with someone (anyone). List the things for which you were grateful, even as that conflict played out. How might gratitude therapy mend your hurting heart?

_____

_____

_____

9. Isaiah 30:21 says, "And your ears shall hear a word behind you, saying, 'This is the way, walk in it,' when you turn to the right or when you turn to the left" (*ESV*). Think about a time you sensed that God was leading you in some way; maybe it was to not say something, or to wait until your emotions caught up with rational thinking. Describe that time here.

_____

_____

_____

_____

_____

_____

10. Did you pause to listen to your Helper? Why or why not?

_____

_____

_____

_____

11. How would it have helped if you had?

_____

_____

_____

_____

12. In what ways do you sense that Jesus wants to help you in your choice points?

_____

_____

_____

_____

_____

THE MENDED HEART PRINCIPLE #9:
YOU MAKE CHOICES AND YOUR CHOICES MAKE YOU

You have an Advocate, Counselor and
Helper in your choice points.

PRAYER

Jesus, my choice points matter to You because I matter to You. Thank You for living inside of me, close as a spoken word or a call for help. I will never be perfect, and You do not ask that of me. But my choices do impact my heart, and the hearts of others. Thank You that I can partner with You in those choice points. Make me aware of them. Teach me to be happy, and to practice gratitude until it becomes a natural part of who I am.

MENDED HEART CHALLENGE

• Look at the 5,000 choices you made yesterday. List those that took a great deal of energy. How important were these choices?
• How did they impact others, whether loved ones or strangers?
• Invite the Holy Spirit in to help you in today's choice points.

Notes
1. Shauna Niequist, *Cold Tangerines* (Grand Rapids, MI: Zondervan, 2007), pp. 234-235.
2. Ibid., p. 17.
3. Ann Morton Voskamp, *One Thousand Gifts* (Grand Rapids, MI: Zondervan, 2010), p. 139.
4. Steve Jobs, Stanford Commencement Address, *Stanford Report*, June 14, 2005. http://news.stanford.edu/news/2005/june15/jobs-061505.html (accessed October 2013).
5. Suzanne Eller, *The Unburdened Heart* (Ventura, CA: Regal Books, 2013), pp. 152-153.
6. "Leslie Vernick, 'Lord, I Want to Be Happy'—Radio Podcast," Encouragement Café, August 23, 2013. http://www.encouragementcafe.com/2013/08/23/leslie-vernick-lord-i-want-to-be-happy-radio-podcast/ (accessed October 2013).

10

Living in Him

God is most glorified in us when we are most satisfied in Him.

JOHN PIPER, *DESIRING GOD*[1]

I'm not sure of the day or even the year when I started calling myself "whole." Like one season passing into another, I shed old ways of thinking, and new ideas and behaviors pushed up through the soil. Sometimes I was surprised at the confidence or ease with which I connected with others, or bravely stepped out of my comfort zone—not realizing until later that it was courageous. There were moments when I listened to someone trapped in the past, and I realized with gratitude how little power my own past now held.

My first high school reunion was enlightening. Richard and I walked up the sidewalk in front of Will Rogers High School, three sets of little hands clutched between us. As I walked up the steps into the building, I was reminded how far God had brought me in just 10 years. The girl who had roamed the halls of Will Rogers worked two jobs. She hung out with friends, went to church and learned about her new faith. She loved Jesus but didn't know very much about the Bible. She drove a fast Mustang and made all the payments herself, as well as the insurance and gas.

She sometimes said dumb things, partly because of her age, but mostly out of a lack of self-confidence. She would then spend the next hour beating herself up emotionally. Those gaffes made her shrink back from putting herself anywhere near the limelight.

She loved her siblings and her parents, but much of the time she also hated her family, because of the conflict. She hated intervening and trying to be the peacemaker. She hated being punished for things that she didn't feel deserved punishment. She hated words that were intended to wound, for her heart was sensitive, and those words dug their way in and settled in like old friends.

She hated being skinny, and having psoriasis. She hated it when people were unkind to each other, especially those who were supposed to love.

Ten years later, all that was my past. The little hands holding on to mine, and the man walking beside me, were my today. Even more importantly, the Jesus I had encountered at 15 had become my heartbeat. Rather than revolving around the things I hated, my life now centered on the fact that I loved Him more than I had ever thought possible.

He lived in me even back in my high school days, but something profound had transpired over those 10 years, and it continues today. I had discovered what it meant for me to live *in* Him.

And that changes everything.

THE JESUS FACTOR

"Therefore if anyone is *in Christ*, he is a new creature; the old things passed away; behold, new things have come" (2 Cor. 5:17, *NASB*, emphasis added).

This verse of Scripture is often associated with how Jesus cleanses our sin and makes us new. While that is true, Paul is talking about life. About ministry. About difficult people. About being misunderstood at times. In this chapter, he's just being straight-up honest about how he felt on some days:

There are times when I get tired.

There are times when people misunderstand my zeal, though I'm trying to do the right thing.

There are times when people hurt me, or make my job hard.

There are times when I feel spiritually empty.

He doesn't end on this dismal thought, however. He moves his focus from those things to Jesus, thus tipping the balance from spiritually tanked out to filling back up.

That's what took place in my life. It's also what God is doing (or desires to accomplish) in yours.

In *THE MESSAGE*, 2 Corinthians 5:17 comes to life:

Now we look inside, and what we see is that anyone united with the Messiah gets a fresh start, is created new. The old life is gone; a new life burgeons!

Don't you love the word "burgeons"? It means to spill out or over, exploding with newness. Prospering. Flourishing. Multiplying!

We started this journey together with the work already completed on the cross. We end it (which just creates a new beginning) with living in Him.

WHAT DOES IT MEAN TO LIVE IN HIM?

To be *in Him* or *in Christ* is a common theme in Scripture. The concept appears in the New Testament more than 70 times! It's a phrase that can be easily overlooked, when it's meant to be internalized instead.

To be in Him is to be united with Christ. It's like a recipe. Flour + lard = pie crust (or so I've heard). Blue + yellow = green. You + in Him = new.

This combination of ingredients brings forth something fresh and new as old thoughts, principles and practices pass away.

I almost laugh now, thinking about how grown up I felt at my 10-year reunion—because my thirty-fifth is approaching soon. Take everything I talked about God doing inside of me in those first 10 years and multiply it by 7 and then 7 more, and it still does not accurately describe who I have become in Him in the decades since then. Maybe this process has just begun for you. You are united with Christ, and old things are starting to pass away. I hope that you celebrate that first day, first week, first month and first year, all the while understanding that there's much more ahead. There's never a stopping point in mending.

If you've been a Christian for a long time, and healing has always felt just beyond your reach, my prayer is that you will discover the *new* in your faith all over again. Pastor J. D. Greear, in his book *Gospel*, describes what happened when this took place in his life:

> It's not that I didn't understand or believe the gospel before. I did. But the truth of the gospel hadn't moved from my mind to my heart. There was a huge gap between my intellect and my emotions. The Puritan Jonathan Edwards likened his reawakening to the gospel to a man who had known, in his head, that honey was sweet, but for the first time had that sweetness burst alive in his mouth. That is what happened to me.
>
> "Rediscovering" the gospel has given me a joy in God I never experienced in all my years of fervent religion.[2]

Living in Him is internalizing what it means for us to unite with Christ. It moves us from a head knowledge to living out the gospel with a heart knowledge.

WHEN YOU LIVE IN HIM, YOU DON'T GIVE UP

Last week you celebrated a victory, but yesterday you felt those same old feelings again. Living in Him (united with Christ) means that you were united with Him when you twirled in your living room because you felt so joyful—and you are also united with Him today when darkness is pressing in around the edges.

> But as many as received Him, to them He gave the right to become children of God, to those who believe in His name (John 1:12, *NKJV*).

All He asks is that you receive Him, and then hold fast to that gift each day. It is Jesus who gives you the right to be called His. It's not about the moment anymore, but the momentum. So reflect and count the ways that He has healed your heart so far. Hold tight to Him on the harder days. You believe *in His* name, and that is your heritage as a child of God.

WHEN YOU LIVE IN HIM, YOUR IDENTITY CHANGES

Let's look at this recipe one more time: you + in Him = new. As you grow closer to God (living in Him), you become more *like* Him.

That's something I didn't realize one week into my faith. It's something I later grasped and delighted in. But it's also something I might forget 35 years in. This isn't like the pictures of people who come to resemble their spouse (or their dog) after a half decade of marriage. It's a heart thing, of course! You start to take on the character of the God who lives inside of you.

The apostle Paul walked into a city where people were desperately trying to figure out matters of faith. They had lots of idols and structures to worship, but they hadn't landed on any one religion. Paul told them that their confusion stemmed from trying to serve gods made by a mere human's hands. He described a living God like this:

> The God who made the world and everything in it is the Lord of heaven and earth and does not live in temples built by human hands. And he is not served by human hands, as if he needed anything. Rather, he himself gives everyone life and breath and everything else. From one man he made all the nations, that they should inhabit the whole earth; and he marked out their appointed times in history and the boundaries of their lands. God did this so that they would seek him and perhaps reach out for him and find him, though he is not far from any one of us. "For in him we live and move and have our being." As some of your own poets have said, "We are his offspring" (Acts 17:24-28).

In Him we live (exist).
In Him we breathe (take in life).
In Him we have our being (our identity).

The more we live in Him—not just going to church, but uniting with God in all aspects of life—the more we start to accept and look for the reality of His presence in the everyday. We see it in us. We see it in the way we interact with others. It is part of the way we think, and it guides the choices we make.

This creates a paradigm shift—a fundamental change in the way we look at something or someone.

For example, Carol, whom we met in Chapter Two, is still aware that her husband left her, but as she lives in Christ, she sees the reality of His presence as she laughs with her daughter. She senses it as she opens the door of her heart to a possible new relationship. She finds her identity in Christ when she's comforted, encouraged or led by the Spirit of God within her, despite what another human being does or does not do. She looks in the mirror, and the woman she sees looking back at her is a child of God with a purpose—not a woman whose husband checked out because of his own issues.

When that takes place, all the shackles come off.

I have come to set free the captive.

Regardless of the brokenness that led you to pick up this book, as you begin to live in Him, you aren't limited anymore. You no longer feel the need to find your identity in another person, or in success, or in the dregs at the bottom of a glass, or in doing more. You don't hide in shame, but find confidence in Whose you are. You start to see the past as just a fragment of who you are.

You anticipate what God is teaching you, and where that knowledge will lead.

But, Suzie, I don't feel all of those things!

I didn't either. Some of them were concrete milestones along the way. Others surprised me. Some continue to unfold in my life. This is not a sprint. It's a marathon, and we can choose to enjoy every mile. The finish line is ahead, but that's not our focus.

Running the race is our goal.

When You Live in Him, God Is Bigger

Nothing we can do actually makes God bigger, but when we live in Him, we start to glimpse the bigness of who He is. As believers, we have often made God small, as we try to fit Him into a box of our making. If we could only grasp how high, how wide, how measureless God is, it would change the face of modern-day Christianity.

We can grab hold of this truth for ourselves, believing that "everything else is worthless when compared with the infinite value of knowing Christ Jesus my Lord" (Phil. 3:8, *NLT*).

When we place a value on knowing Christ, rather than thinking that we know everything there is to know about a situation or a person—or even ourselves—we start to see things through the eyes of our heavenly Father. This knowledge becomes conviction (a set of beliefs), which translates into our character, which changes us and the way we approach life.

It also changes the way others see the bigness of Jesus.

It's our Heart Surgeon at His finest, as Jesus' mission fills us up and becomes a part of our being, in such a measure that it not only changes us, but also has the power to impact those in proximity to us. For 30-plus years, these words of Paul have been a prayer for my life, and now they are my prayer for you as well:

> I pray that out of his glorious riches he may strengthen you with power through his Spirit *in your inner being*, so that Christ may dwell *in your hearts* through faith. And I pray that you, being rooted and established in love, may have power, together with all the Lord's holy people, to grasp how wide and long and high and deep is the love of Christ, and to know this love that surpasses knowledge—that you may be filled to the measure of all the fullness of God.
>
> Now to him who is able to do immeasurably more than all we ask or imagine, according to his power that *is at work within us*, to him be glory in the church and

in Christ Jesus throughout all generations, for ever and ever! Amen (Eph. 3:16-21, emphasis added).

WHEN YOU LIVE IN HIM, YOU GET HUNGRY

I just ate a Subway sandwich, whole wheat chips, and a white chocolate macadamia nut cookie. If you tried to give me something to eat at this moment, I'd turn you down, no matter how good it smelled or looked.

The theory in physical hunger is this: The more you eat, the fuller you become and the less you want.

That's the exact opposite of how spiritual hunger works.

Maybe you know something is missing. You want to connect with God, but you are waiting to "feel it." So you don't pick up the Bible. You don't spend time with God alone, or if you do, you approach it as a task: Get in there. Get out. Check! It's off the list.

The principle of spiritual hunger is this: The more you eat, the hungrier you get.

Stormie Omartian, in *Finding Peace for Your Heart*, recounts how she once prayed for relief from her anxious thoughts. Her pastor recommended reading the Bible. While the teaching always seemed clear when someone else explained the Bible, Stormie feared that the Scriptures would be hard to read and understand on her own—but she longed for help, so she plunged in anyway. She read a psalm and a proverb each morning, and then read again at night before she went to sleep.

Within weeks she looked forward to that time of reflection, and after a year of reading the Bible each morning and each night, she was able to report, "Gradually the Bible became God's voice in my ear."[3]

The spiritual hunger principle had kicked in. She hadn't been hungry in the beginning, but she took a few bites—and then a few more bites—out of obedience. As she continued consuming the Word, she started filling up, which made her hungrier. She started to experience God's voice and direction.

Which made her hungrier still.

In Hebrews 4:12, we read the word *heart*, but that's not the emphasis. Rather the author is placing the weight on the words leading up to it, sharing that God's Word has the power to affect the condition or **attitude** (*ennoia*) of the heart. When *ennoia* occurs, it enlarges your ability to think well.

Hebrews 4:12 says:

God's Word is living and powerful. It is sharper than a sword that cuts both ways. It cuts straight into where the soul and spirit meet and it divides them. It cuts into the joints and bones. It tells what the heart is thinking about and what it wants to do (*NLV*).

As you begin to meet with Jesus daily, the stories and teachings of the Bible will cut straight through to the core of who you are—both the impulsive, human nature and that part of you that is God-breathed, God-filled and God-purposed.

Please don't make this a task.

It's not a test that you fail.

Perhaps it's taking one Scripture verse or passage and meditating on it and studying it for a week. It might be writing down a verse on a note card and carrying that card with you throughout the day. Maybe it's picking up a great devotional and delving into the insights contained within, side by side with the Bible and a journal.

This has been a daily mini-massage to my heart for over three decades. Most mornings I read my favorite daily devotional or a few pages in a book like this. Then I open my Bible with pen in hand and study a small portion of Scripture. I may memorize a verse, or journal something that I learned, or think about an idea that the Holy Spirit brought to mind.

I listen to worship music, but you'll do it your way. My thoughts tend to careen at times, and soft worship music centers me.

There's no time clock on this, because we don't put a time restriction on the relationships we hold most dear.

The time you spend in His presence and in the Word will gradually change how you think, which changes who you are in your thoughts, which will begin to reflect the words of Jesus imprinted on your heart.

It also helps you to hear His voice.

When I first became a Christian, I didn't know what that meant. Over time, I learned that it's something that happens on the inside of us. God reveals truth to us through His Spirit as the deeper things of God are weighed. For me, it's a hammering of my heart when I'm about to take a step in the wrong direction. Sadly, sometimes it's the conviction I experience after I plowed past that feeling and did it anyway.

Or it's a pause that says "slow down," giving my emotions a moment to catch up with right thinking.

Sometimes it's a green light. I'm supposed to go, do, act, think big, or walk in faith.

JESUS' MISSION IN YOU

Here we are at the end of our journey together. But really it's just the start. You are engaged in a relationship with Christ that reflects the life of the Spirit. You are walking with Him, following His lead. Your focus is not on the past or another person, or even a set of circumstances, though your story matters to God very much. Your life is distinguished by a focus on Jesus lovingly leading you from broken to whole.

You are breaking the patterns of the past. You are no longer doing what you've always done, or thinking the way you always thought. You are branching out of your comfort zone, even if it feels scary, because "He's got you, sis. He's got you."

You are worried less about being a smashing success or a poster child for "pull yourself up by your bootstraps" theology, and you have placed your faith in a partnership with Jesus as you take one step forward, and then another, praising God for every small victory you experience in Him.

His mission statement lives *in you*.

Jesus brought good news to you and you received it.

Jesus was sent to release the captives and you held up your shackles.

Jesus opened your blinded eyes so that you might see things differently.

Your heart was once broken, but now it's free, free, free.

JUST *You* AND *God*

1. When your heart begins to mend, it's a new beginning. What might that mean to you?

   _____
   _____
   _____
   _____

2. Mending is a lifelong process. At times you will struggle. Read Hebrews 4:15-16. What does Jesus offer in those struggles?

   _____
   _____
   _____
   _____

3. Compare spiritual hunger with physical hunger. Then consider ways you might start feeding your spirit. What does that look like for you?

   _____
   _____
   _____
   _____

4. What new things do you feel stirring inside of you? Have you taken time to celebrate those? Share the good news about God's work in you with someone today.

   _____
   _____
   _____
   _____

5. Maybe you think there's still too much you don't know about Jesus. What can happen, according to 1 John 2:27, as you begin to grow in your faith?

_____

_____

_____

6. What is your fear about tomorrow? Speak it out loud.

_____

_____

_____

7. Read Psalm 147:1-5. This is the psalmist's praise. He wrote it when he was both hopeful and afraid. He praised God in the midst of challenging circumstances. Write your own psalm of praise. Read it out loud.

_____

_____

_____

8. How powerful is it to have your fears quieted with hope in Jesus?

_____

_____

_____

The Mended Heart Principle #10:
You Live and Move and Have Your Being in Him

He lives in you, but you are also invited to live *in Him*.

Prayer

Jesus, Your mission statement is coming alive in me. I know we have a long way to go together, but look how far we've come in such a short time. Hope flickered, and now it's flaming. I don't have all the answers, but I have You! Thank You that I can live and move and have my being in You. Thank You for a mended heart.

Mended Heart Challenge

- Create a space and time for intimacy with Christ. It's not about the number of minutes, but the relationship.
- Connect with others (this could be through a small group, a church, a neighborhood Bible study, or some other way).
- Go back and read your first week's answers. What have you learned over the past few weeks?

Notes
1. John Piper, *Desiring God* (Colorado Springs, CO: Multnomah Books, 2011), p. 10. See also http://www.desiringgod.org/resource-library/ask-pastor-john/how-is-the-statement-god-is-most-glorified-in-us-when-we-are-most-satisfied-in-him-true-for-those-who-wont-be-saved (accessed October 2013).
2. J. D. Greear, *Gospel: Rediscovering the Power That Made Christianity Revolutionary* (Nashville, TN: B&H Publishing Group, 2011), p. 4.
3. Stormie Omartian, *Finding Peace for Your Heart* (Nashville, TN: Thomas Nelson, 1999), p. 33.

$Q \ \& \ A$

Several women came alongside me as I wrote *The Mended Heart*. I also shared questions with women in my Facebook community (at https://www.facebook.com/SuzanneEllerP31) and on Twitter. Here are a few of the questions that came up as we discussed what it might look like to have a mended heart. Maybe these are questions you've asked as well.

Q: I'm in the process of healing, but the person who caused my brokenness isn't. He is a family member, so he will always be in my life. How do I effectively set boundaries without holding resentment toward this person?

A: Boundaries are not intended to punish, but are a tool to work toward the healthiest relationship possible within your individual circumstances. For example, if you have an alcoholic parent, punishing them would be cutting them out of your life forever in anger and to make them pay for how they hurt you. Boundaries that are intended to work toward healing might look like this: "If you call drunk, we can't talk, but I'd love to talk with you sober." "My children can't be alone with you or in a car with you because of an alcohol problem, but we'll meet you at the park." "If a conversation degenerates into a trip down a destructive or harmful path, we'll politely leave, but I'll honor you with my words, for I won't do what I'm asking you not to do." ("If it is possible, as far as it depends on you, live at peace with everyone" [Rom. 12:18].)

Q: How do I let go of past hurts? Will I ever be okay?

A: The process begins with surrendering to all that God has for you. It starts right there. When you surrender, you don't have all the answers. There's not even a clear plan at this point. You just know that you are tired of battling this on your own.

You aren't sure where He's going to take you, you aren't sure what He's going to ask you to do, and you aren't sure what you'll look like whole; you just know that you need Him to walk through it with you.

So you surrender your thoughts, your hurts, the deep secrets, the pain, the anger, the things you hate, and the things you love that aren't good for you. You surrender all of this daily until healthier thoughts, healing, openness, peace and new direction start to move in. Surrendering is the first step—just the beginning—but it's a powerful step. Surrendering is not a weak word. In Scriptures like James 4:7, it means to subject your whole life to God. You are placing it in bigger hands. Thus surrendering becomes a strong partnership with your God, who loves you.

Will you ever be okay? Yes, ma'am. I don't know exactly what that will look like, but I pray it's more than you ever hoped. Just start the journey, and see where God will take you. ("Submit yourselves, then, to God. Resist the devil, and he will flee from you" [Jas. 4:7].)

Q: I struggle to trust people. So, even though I am a believer, I don't let people in. Can't I just do this mending process by myself?

A: Flying solo is only fun if you are on an airplane, and even then having a co-pilot is a good idea. But let's be honest, when you've been hurt, the last thing you may want to seek out is friendships or other close relationships. But what if the answer to your prayer—for encouragement, for wisdom, for a new way of looking at life—is waiting in the form of a friend, a group, a church, a Bible study or a neighbor?

You may be waiting for someone to reach out to you. This is understandable, but it's also limiting. The people God may desire to place in your life might not be wandering down your street. So, rather than waiting for someone to come to you, you reach out. That might be in a small group at church, or a Celebrate Recovery group (http://www.celebraterecovery.com/) in your community, or a volunteer group that helps others in your area.

Will the people you connect with be perfect? No. People are fallible. But as you expand your reach to include new people in your circle, you start to appreciate the differences in potential friendships. You give friendship or church another opportunity if you've been hurt. Rather than looking or waiting for others to meet your needs (which isn't the goal of friendship), you simply connect. ("That is, that you and I may be mutually encouraged by each other's faith" [Rom. 1:12].)

Q: Why didn't you share more details of your story in The Mended Heart?

A: Because my old story isn't my story anymore. It's a small part of it—a chapter. And every time I go into detail about my childhood, I have to take into account that my beautiful mom is going to read it. She carries my books with her and hands them out to friends. She loves what Jesus has done. But it's never easy to relive the hurts or mistakes of the past, especially when you've changed. Our story is shared in *The Unburdened Heart* and *The Mom I Want to Be*, and briefly on my blog (www.tsuzanneeller. com), but today I delight in telling the world that my mom is my friend, and I adore her.

In fact, I'd love to write her story one day! It's a powerful testimony to what God can do in the midst of brokenness. I pray she'll let me write it.

Bottom line, while I allude to the feelings and hurts of the past in *The Mended Heart*, I love sharing what Jesus has done and can do, rather than telling an old story one more time.

Q: Is my heart hurt because of something I need to forgive in myself, or something I need to forgive in someone else?

A: This is a profound question. Let's begin with the issue of forgiving yourself.

Genuine remorse is a beautiful thing. But the act of forgiving oneself isn't found in Scripture. Rather, we are asked to receive what God offers freely: to remove our sins far from us. "For as high as the heavens are above the earth, so great is his love for those who fear him; as far as the east is from the west, so far has he removed our transgressions from us" (Ps. 103:11-12).

What a beautiful, overwhelming extension of grace! We can sincerely apologize and make amends, but this promise allows us to stop carrying around something that God has already covered with His atonement.

If your heart is hurt because you need to forgive someone else, that too is possible with God's help. So, regardless of which one it is, a work of forgiveness takes place inside of you. As I shared in *The Unburdened Heart*, forgiving isn't a one-dimensional word. It's not just an act or a will or a thought. It's leaving one place to find another. It's allowing God to move into the raw wounds and broken places. It's a new identity and a fresh start. It's getting out of the debt-collection business. I hope you'll check out *The Unburdened Heart* to help you begin this multi-layered journey toward forgiving. It's something we are privileged to do, for it absolutely leads to freedom from the burden of unforgiveness and bitterness.

Q: *How do I make the broken places in my heart understand what my mind knows to be true?*

A: I love this question. I hear the heart of someone who is holding tight to truth but who is still in the healing process. Can we take just a moment and celebrate that? You are aware that there are broken places. You aren't denying them. You aren't hiding them. You are reaching for truth! That's faith! That's courage.

In the last chapter, we discussed living *in Him*. One way to live in Him is to celebrate every small step forward that you take as a result of being united with Christ. I meet many women who stand in front of me trembling, tears running down their faces. They start to tell me the work that still needs to be done. I respect that so much, and we will take time to pray and talk, but we always pause first to reflect on how far they've come.

Most of them have never given themselves a pat on the back or an atta-girl, or even stopped to praise God for those huge leaps forward. Why not? Because the changes may seem small to others, or the women suffered a couple of falls in between, or the finish line seems so far away. But any time you're climbing a mountain, you have to stop from time to time and look at the view behind you to appreciate how far you've come.

When you start to celebrate those ascending moments, truth settles in your heart. You see what you and God have done together. You stop looking at the end goal and start looking at the next step instead, but with a firm knowledge of how far you've come already! That's exciting! ("Finally, brothers and sisters, whatever is true, whatever is noble, whatever is right, whatever is pure, whatever is lovely, whatever is admirable—if

anything is excellent or praiseworthy—think about such things"
[Phil. 4:8].)

Q: Why am I here?

A: Your question came to me on Twitter (www.twitter.com/
suzanneeller). I saved it for last, because I want the answer to linger
in the hearts of those who read it. You are here because you matter
to God. Perhaps people have told you differently, or there's a lie you
have come to believe—like that you are unworthy or have no merit.
I could easily ask this same question, for I was conceived as a result
of sexual assault by my mother's estranged husband. Things were
hard when I was growing up, because the people around me were
hurting, and that affected us all. But regardless of the way I entered
the world, or the brokenness that surrounded me, God delighted
in me. He delights in you, too. Psalm 139:13-14 says, "For you
created my inmost being; you knit me together in my mother's
womb. I praise you because I am fearfully and wonderfully made;
your works are wonderful, I know that full well."

You and I are His works. God knows that this world and many
of the people in it have tried to go on without Him. The Bible
describes Him as reaching for us. When we reach back, we begin
to discover who we really are, and why we are here.

God desires to transform us from the inside out. Not to make
us a clone, or to change our personality, but to bring together the
Creator and His creation. Knowing Him is a lifetime of trusting
and walking with God.

I still sometimes stop and ask, "Why am I here?" But it's no
longer a question that seeps from pain. Rather, it's an excited
response to a new day. "Lord, why am I here today—in this place,
and with these people? What do You want to show me, or do
through me?"

My prayer is that you will grab hold of Jesus' mission statement and walk toward healing, knowing that Jesus is in you and with you today. If the Christian faith is new to you, it's simple.

We are only asked to believe that Jesus is Lord (see Rom. 10:9; Acts 16:31; John 3:15). Do you believe? If so, today you begin to walk with Him—to discover what it means to be a follower of Christ and a woman absolutely loved by her *Abba* Father.

About Suzanne Eller

Suzie (as friends call her) is passionate about coming alongside women and leading them in a new direction in the areas of family, feelings and faith. Suzie is an author and international speaker with Proverbs 31 Ministries.

She is a cancer survivor and lives life to the fullest.

She is a mom, wife and gramma who lives in beautiful green country—Oklahoma. When Suzie is not writing or speaking, you'll find her hiking, running 5Ks, tending her garden or rafting down a river. If you are interested in having Suzie be a keynote speaker or address your church or women's conference on this or other topics, please contact Proverbs 31 Ministries.

Connect with Suzanne (Suzie)

If you have grown in your faith, or God is doing a work in your heart, or you just need someone to pray with you, I'd love to hear from you. Contact me at:

www.tsuzanneeller.com/contact.
www.facebook.com/SuzanneEllerP31
www.twitter.com/suzanneeller.

If *The Mended Heart* is helping you heal in your broken places, please tell others. I write and speak because I love watching what only God can do. When you spread the word, you partner with me in this and I'm grateful.

You can do this by sharing the book with a friend, or by placing this copy in a library or gifting it to a women's ministry. You can begin a Bible study in your church or neighborhood or small group.

You can also leave reviews, which help others discern whether this is a book they want to read. That helps more than you'll ever know! You can do that at:

http://www.amazon.com/Mended-Heart-Healing-Broken-
Places/dp/0830767819/

http://www.barnesandnoble.com/w/the-mended-heart-
suzanne-eller/1115249764?ean=9780830767816

If you share about this book on your blog, or are hosting a Bible study on *The Mended Heart*, drop me a note (www.tsuzanneeller.com/contact) and perhaps I can drop in via Skype or FaceTime, or leave a comment on your blog for your readers. I'd love that!

Proverbs 31
MINISTRIES

If you were inspired by *The Mended Heart,* and you desire to deepen your own personal relationship with Jesus Christ, I encourage you to connect with Proverbs 31 Ministries.

Proverbs 31 Ministries exists to be a trusted friend that will take you by the hand and walk by your side, leading you one step closer to the heart of God through these resources:

- *Encouragement for Today* online daily devotions
- The *P31 Woman* monthly magazine
- Daily radio program
- Books and resources
- Dynamic speakers with life-changing messages
- Online Bible studies
- Gather and Grow Groups and online communities

To learn more about Proverbs 31 Ministries, or to inquire about having Suzanne Eller speak at your event, call 1-877-731-4663 or visit www.proverbs31.org.

Proverbs 31 Ministries
630 Team Road, Suite 100
Matthews, NC 28105
www.Proverbs31.org